S·A·L·M·O·N C·A·M·P

The Boland Brook Story

65 Years of Angling on the Upsalquitch River

by **LIVINGSTON PARSONS, Jr.**

Frank Amato

PORTLAND

Praise for Salmon Camp

"The classic, rustic Canadian salmon camp has always been an enchanted place, touched only incidentally by the hue-and-cry of the modern, mechanized world. The very model for that kind of camp is Boland Brook, that fabulous square mile of New Brunswick bisected by one of the continent's great salmon rivers, the Upsalquitch. In this book, *Salmon Camp*, Livy Parsons brings you into this realm with its eccentric assortment of characters, tumbling rapids and towering pines and leaping, silver salmon."

Peter Bodo, Outdoors columnist, *The New York Times*

*   *   *   *   *   *

"In the 1920's Edward Hewitt fished the Upsalquitch in New Brunswick with George Labranche and Ambrose Monell. The account of their research and their experiences with the dry fly covered the subject thoroughly and are still famous. In 1936 a determined New York young lady, Katharine deB. Parsons, bought a square mile on the very same river, around Boland Brook, and built a beautiful camp there.

Livy Parsons was eleven years old when he was invited to fish for his first Atlantic salmon. For the next sixty-six years he continued to vacation at Boland Brook Camp. He has written its story and recounted how it has been preserved in its original charm and romantic beauty.

Livy is a 'compleat' salmon angler, a staunch conservationist and chair of the Research Committee, Atlantic Salmon Federation. His story is unique; it's a small jewel that every salmon fisher will discover with joy."

Lucien Rolland, Past President, Atlantic Salmon Federation (Canada)

*   *   *   *   *   *

"Livy Parsons' engrossing chronicle of his family's salmon camp over several generations is also the saga of the Atlantic salmon, The King of Game Fish."

Robert Berls, Editor of "The Anglers' Club Bulletin"

Katharine deB. Parsons, 1972.

Dedicated to the memory of Katharine deB. Parsons.
1898-1993

Without her spirit of adventure, attention to detail
and refusal to always accept conventional thoughts,
the events in this book would never have occurred
and the book would not have been written.

Author, age 20 and Katharine deB. Parsons on the
front steps at Boland Brook Camp.

This book is based on a series of eleven articles published between 1997 and 2002 in "The Anglers' Club Bulletin" of the Anglers' Club of New York, 101 Broad Street, New York, N.Y., 10004.

Acknowledgements

For their help and encouragement in bringing this book to completion, my thanks to:

Peter Bodio, outdoor columnist for *The New York Times*;

Fred Whoriskey, Vice President for Research and Environment of the Atlantic Salmon Federation;

Jack Samson, fly-fisherman, writer and editor;

Frank Amato and Kim Koch of Frank Amato Publications

and most of all Joan Parsons for her enthusiastic support, suggestions and technical help with preparation of the manuscript.

All inquiries should be addressed to:
Frank Amato Publications, Inc.
P.O. Box 82112 • Portland, Oregon 97282
503-653-8108 • www.amatobooks.com

Book Design: Amy Tomlinson
All photos are the property of Livingston Parsons, Jr., unless otherwise noted.

Hardbound Limited ISBN: 1-57188-327-4
Hardbound Limited UPC: 0-81127-00161-3

Softbound ISBN: 1-57188-336-3
Softbound UPC: 0-81127-00170-5

Printed in Singapore
1   3   5   7   9   10   8   6   4   2

TABLE OF
CONTENTS

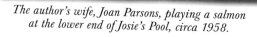

A typical morning's catch in 1939, 7 salmon and 3 grilse.

*The author's wife, Joan Parsons, playing a salmon
at the lower end of Josie's Pool, circa 1958.*

FOREWORD

by Wilfred Carter
THE BOLAND BROOK STORY

*T*he Upsalquitch River, in northern New Brunswick, Canada, is a twenty-four mile-long, gin-clear tributary of the famed Restigouche, entering the river about fourteen miles from its mouth, near Campbellton, N.B. Atlantic salmon ascend the river from the sea in late June and remain in the pools until late October or early November, when they spawn to produce a new generation of young salmon. At two or three years of age the young salmon move out to sea, to grow and fatten, for a year or more before return-ing to the river where they are eagerly awaited by anglers who claim that the Atlantic salmon is the greatest freshwater game fish that swims. An addicted salmon angler, as most are or are soon to become, is truly mad, and will go to the ends of the earth to cast a fly over a favorite salmon pool, in the hope of seeing a bolt of silver lightning erupt from beneath the artificial fly in an acrobatic display that has no equal. Sadly, the Atlantic salmon has not fared well over the past several decades, suffering declines caused by over-fishing, environmental degradation, dams, aquaculture, and other asso-ciated problems. Salmon runs on most Atlantic salmon rivers have been much below historic levels. However, there is brighter hope for the future, as organizations like the Atlantic Salmon Federation strive to reverse the fortune of the wild Atlantic salmon.

Dr. Livingston Parsons has written a fascinating story about his aunt, Katharine deB. Parsons' adventures in purchasing a square mile of forest and more than a mile of salmon fishing property, located along the Upsalquitch River, in northern New Brunswick. The property title had its origin through a Royal Grant by King William IV in 1836. Katharine, or Allie, as she was known to the author and his two sisters, Miss Parsons to everyone else, purchased the property after a brief visit to inspect it in 1936, and spent every summer there until her death in 1993. Livy recounts the many details of the building and operation of Boland Brook Camp with a surgeon's attention to accuracy and completeness, but above all else this is a story of a feisty and intrepid lady who knew exactly what she wanted and brooked no interference with her well-laid plans from anyone, even her much-loved nephew.

To appreciate the enormous scale of the undertaking, one needs to know that the property Miss Parsons bought in 1936 was located twelve miles from the nearest settlement, the last four accessible only by canoe. After purchasing the property, this extraordinary single lady undertook the design and placement of a lodge and other buildings on the property, only engaging an architect to prepare final working drawings, and supervised every minute detail of their construction, completed in 1937. All of the lumber, construction materials and every last nail needed for the job had to be hauled up to the Boland Brook site on a flat-bottomed scow, propelled by real horse power—the four-legged kind.

Only a person of extraordinary skill and determination would undertake such a formidable challenge, and Miss Parsons possessed those attributes, in spades. Resolute and austere, to most people she was an intimidating presence. You didn't argue with Miss Parsons; there was only one way to accomplish a task and that was usually Miss Parsons' way, and woe-betide anyone who thought his or her way was better. As her nephew, Livy, expresses it, "arbitration wasn't her long suit." My wife, Pauline, got a classic introduction to Miss Parsons when we went to Boland Brook as her guests for a few days some years ago. We started out on the wrong foot by arriving late, a mortal sin in Miss Parsons' book, and after a frosty reception, with barely time to down a quick gin and tonic, the bell announcing lunch sounded. Pauline stood up and held the screen door open, expecting Miss Parsons to lead the way, but instead, she whacked Pauline across the backside with her cane, while admonishing her to hurry up as she was letting in hordes of blackflies!

Miss Parsons died in 1993; she had spent 57 summers at Boland Brook, enjoying every minute. The Boland Brook property is owned today by her nephew, Dr. Livingston Parsons, but little has changed. It is still isolated, beautiful and serene. The alarm clock is still sounded by the slamming screen door announcing another day in a corner of paradise, where one needs to worry only about the choice of fly that will successfully attract the salmon. That choice would not have been a problem for Miss Parsons. She would almost certainly have selected a Fuzzy Wuzzy, the fly she created as her "secret weapon", and wouldn't even show to Clovis Arsenault, the local fly-tying maestro.

Dr. Parsons enhances the story of Boland Brook by recounting some personal experiences during the times he and his family spent there, in encounters with poachers, forest fires, prospectors and bureaucrats. The portraits he paints, especially in the situations where Miss Parsons is directly involved, like the confrontation with the giant mining company, Noranda, are at times hilarious and revealing.

Livy's opinions on fishing tactics and salmon management are sure to arouse readers' curiosity and even their scepticism. His sharply critical views on native fishing and government inactivity to address salmon management issues will elicit positive endorsement. Dr. Parsons' advice to "get your fly in the water", if you want to ensure fishing success, and his admonition to go fishing to especially enjoy the beauty of the forest and the rivers and the companionship of friends, is timely and touching.

Wilfred M. Carter
17th November, 2003

Boland Brook Camp

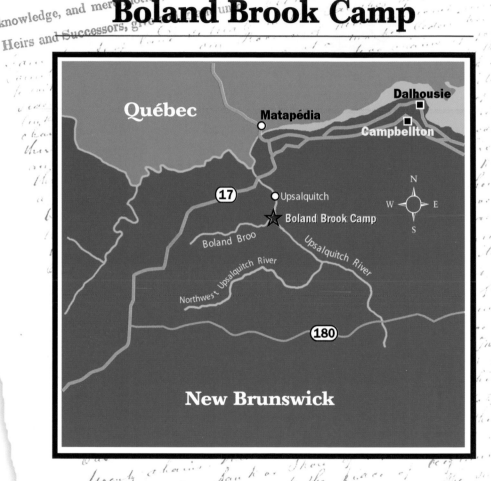

C H A P T E R

The Beginning

From 1936 to 1993 when she died at the age of 96,
Katharine deB. Parsons of New York City owned
and ran Boland Brook Camp, a salmon fishing camp,
on the Upsalquitch River in New Brunswick,
an Atlantic province of Canada.

It was and is a unique fishing camp for several reasons: it was, perhaps, the first and only salmon fishing camp owned and operated by a woman; no guest has ever paid to fish there; and it has remained a small family camp, very different from the more luxurious and larger commercially operated camps with which most salmon anglers of eastern Canada, Europe and Scandinavia are familiar. The camp has never been operated as a club or commercial venture.

When Katharine Parsons died in 1993, the management of Boland Brook Camp became, for the first time, my responsibility. I was not venturing into uncharted waters, since I had been visiting Boland Brook Camp for the past 55 years from 1937 to 1992, missing only three years, two years in 1953 to 1955, while I was serving in the U.S. Army, and my first year of solo surgical practice in New Mexico in 1959, when I was convinced that the few loyal patients I had would leave me, if I were gone, even for a week.

Boland Brook has always been an important part of my life, as it was for my aunt. The camp has an exciting and intensely interesting past and present, remaining a retreat for family and close friends, the latter, providing they are hardcore fishermen. I will explain now, before you chastise me for being politically incorrect (which would not bother me) or outdated (which would), that when I use the term "fisherman" or "fishermen," I am referring to people of either gender. My reasons for feeling this way will be more understandable as you get further into this story. This book chronicles some of Boland Brook Camp's history prior to its purchase by Katharine Parsons in 1936 and events from that date to the present.

Those who fly-fish for Atlantic salmon are passionate, perhaps even irrational at times, about their sport. I know of some who would define us as members of a "cult," hard to appreciate, if you are a non-member. What I am really trying to say is, that this book may not appeal to all who pick it up, but if you are a member of this cult, or just intrigued by cult members you have encountered, you may be less likely to put it down.

Camp Pool at Boland Brook Camp, 1938.

The Restigouche River is one of the historic and most widely known salmon rivers of eastern Canada. Older writings refer to it as "Ristigouche," a word thought by some to have been derived from the word "Listogotch," used by the Mi'kmaq Indians to describe their river. It is one of the three major river systems in New Brunswick, the other two being the Miramichi in eastern New Brunswick and the Saint John in southwest New Brunswick. The Restigouche has established a reputation as one of the prime Atlantic salmon rivers in the world and as a producer of large salmon. The lower Restigouche composes the border between the provinces of Quebec and New Brunswick, flowing from west to east to enter the Bay of Chaleur (chaleur means "heat" in French), a misnomer, if there ever was one. Two of the longest and largest tributaries of the Restigouche are the Matapedia, entering on the Quebec side about three miles from the mouth, and the Upsalquitch, entering on the New Brunswick side. From the mouth of the Restigouche River at the Bay of Chaleur, it is about ten miles to the mouth of the Upsalquitch. Few inhabitants of the area know the meaning or derivation of the word, "Upsalquitch," but Dr. George Frederick Clarke, a New Brunswick historian and archeologist, has stated that it comes from the Mi'kmaq and Maliseet Indian dialects, where "op-set-kwetch" means "narrow going". Personally, I love the sound of the word and am not overly concerned about its translation.

The two major branches of the Upsalquitch River are the Southeast Upsalquitch (known as "the Sou'east") and the larger Northwest Upsalquitch (known as "the Nor'west"). Both branches join to form a large pool at "The Forks," and from there the main Upsalquitch River wanders to the north for 24 miles through some of the most beautiful forest land in eastern Canada to its entry into the Restigouche River at "Camp Harmony." The Upsalquitch remains the most beautiful river on which I have ever fished for salmon, or for any other fish, for that matter. Boland Brook Camp is situated fourteen miles up river from the mouth, still to this day delightfully isolated and inaccessible by road.

Katharine deB. Parsons (1897-1993) was born in New York City and lived there all her life. She and my father grew up in the city and were descendents of several prominent, old New York families, the Delanceys and the Barclays, but it is best not to trace family history too far back, since the first Parsons to reach New York City was Thomas Burrington Parsons (1794-1869), who was a deserter from a British ship in the War of 1812, swimming ashore to hide out in Long Island. After a year, when he thought the coast was clear (literally and figuratively), he established residence in New York City and married Anne Barclay (1788-1869).

Katharine Parsons never married and, as a young woman, lived with her widowed father, Harry deB. Parsons, an engineer who was a recognized authority on steam boilers. She devoted herself to his care and happiness, as her mother had wished. She helped him entertain, when that was necessary and traveled abroad with him, when he was asked to speak at engineering meetings. After his death she lived alone in a Manhattan apartment, actively involving herself with civic endeavors, such as Roosevelt-St. Luke's Hospital, as a Board Member and Volunteer, and with the Canadian Maple Leaf, the Canadian equivalent of the U.S. Red Cross. Boland Brook Camp in Canada was certainly a factor in her involvement with The Maple Leaf and also with an arrangement she had with Abercrombie and Fitch to tie Atlantic salmon flies for resale in their fishing department. Her personal and political inclinations were conservative and her view of the world around her could be described as near Victorian. Children, such as my two sisters and myself, were tolerated in small doses, providing we met her definition of behaving. She was socially shy, bringing little attention to herself, reserved in the presence of people she did not know well, but often outspoken in family affairs and extremely generous and open to her friends. If you crossed her, deceived her or reneged on a promise, you were through and there would be nothing you could do from that point on to get back in her good graces. A verbal consensus or a handshake was enough to cement an agreement and, as far as I can remember, she never failed to keep a promise or a threat. Her spoken word was her bond. She also had an iron will to achieve her goals and to promote her beliefs with action.

Aunt Katharine never believed any reasonable person would live outside a fifty-mile radius, at the farthest, from the Big Apple. Living as I was in Albuquerque, placed me in an awkward category. But why, with this philosophy, would a single woman in her late thirties, living in New York City, buy 640 acres of the New Brunswick woods? For most readers, it is obvious -- for one reason only: Atlantic salmon, that extraordinary creature, The King of Game Fish.

To escape the oppressive heat of New York summers in the days before air-conditioning, Katharine Parsons made annual visits for several years to Nova

Katharine deB. Parsons as a young woman in her late teens or early twenties, circa 1920.

Scotia, where she was introduced to salmon fishing, the beauty of salmon rivers and the interesting personalities of those who guide and fish for the King of Game Fish. Unfortunately, she never caught a salmon. Dr. Ross Faulkner, an ear, nose and throat specialist in New York City, knew my Aunt Katharine and her sinuses (frontal, maxillary and ethmoid) very well. One spring day in 1936, while she was in his office undergoing a somewhat uncomfortable procedure, he attempted to divert her attention by asking, if she would be interested in buying a square mile of the New Brunswick woods. Katharine, who always approached things in a non-devious manner, retorted, "about as much as I would be interested in another hole in my head." (an appropriate commentary, considering the procedure she was undergoing at that moment). Dr. Faulkner's next question was, "Would it make any difference to you, if you knew that a mile and a quarter of one of New Brunswick's best Atlantic salmon rivers ran through this square mile?" She said, "Yes, it certainly would," and this is how it all got started. In a subsequent conversation she learned that some property on the Upsalquitch River, owned by the Black family from Halifax, was for sale and that Watiqua, the Black fishing camp, was available to lease for a week that summer. She placed an option to purchase the 640 acres shortly thereafter and, in addition, leased Watiqua for the week in the coming August. Dr. Faulkner and another friend, Bunny Avery, would join her there for some salmon fishing.

While at Watiqua that summer Katharine learned that there were two separate square miles, either one of which was up for sale, the Watiqua site at Grog Brook and the other more than six miles up river at Boland Brook, or Boland's Brook, as it is called on very old maps. Each block, a square mile of land, was owned by the Black family and both properties had the riparian rights included. Basically having the riparian rights meant that the owner of the land bordering a river had the legal right to control who fished in that area of the river. The river, nonetheless, was a "public highway" and the landowner had no control of travel on the river.

She promptly engaged Allan Murray, a young guide from the settlement of Upsalquitch, to take her up river to see the Boland Brook property. Allan lashed two Gaspé boats together, placed Bunny Avery, Dr. Faulkner and Katharine Parsons therein, and riding on a trusted farm horse, towed the two boats up the river. Gaspé boats were the predecessors of modern-day canoes in New Brunswick and Quebec. Made entirely of wood, they were about the same length as a twenty-two-foot wood and canvas canoe, but a little narrower and the bow and stern slanted in toward the center of the boat to facilitate "poling." The bad news was that Gaspé boats were quite tippy. All the guides of that era and of that generation could stand in the stern of a Gaspé boat using their own hand-hewn spruce pole, eight feet in length with a pointed iron shield on the end, and propel the boat upstream at a steady rate through fast-flowing water, even rapids, for hours at a time with graceful, balanced, repetitive strokes. A second person could pole standing in the bow. For those being transported in this fashion, it was relaxing, almost hypnotic and an ideal way to enjoy deeply beautiful surroundings.

When the party reached Boland Brook, they found a fast-flowing, icy-cold, feeder stream, perhaps twenty-five feet wide, entering the Upsalquitch River on its west bank in one of the few relatively flat areas along the river. The gently sloping area extended back about eighty yards from the river before rising steeply to ridges three to four hundred feet in elevation. Due to a huge forest fire in 1923, which had burned many hundreds of square miles, there were few trees, except along the river banks and the brook, and the land appeared largely barren with only a few scattered young maples and spruces three to six feet high. The land down river from the brook looked perfect for building a fishing camp, and was the deciding factor in selecting this land from the two pieces for sale. A bonus was the view of jumping salmon in the large pool just below the entrance of the brook, a view that necessitated an on-the-spot decision to purchase the property.

The Boland Brook property was it! There was no doubt about it! A momentous decision! Negotiations with the Blacks and legal matters were completed by September 17, 1936, establishing Katharine deB. Parsons as the proud owner of both a square mile of land in the province of New Brunswick as well as riparian rights on more than a mile of a clear, sparkling, pristine salmon river. The purchase price was $12,000 Canadian dollars, less than I paid for a quarter of an acre of land in Albuquerque, New Mexico, in 1958.

Boland Brook, circa 1937.

CHAPTER

2

NEW BRUNSWICK.

WILLIAM the Fourth, by the Grace of GOD, of the
United Kingdom of Great Britain and Ireland, King, Defender
of the Faith, &c. To all to whom these presents shall come,
GREETING: Know ye, that We, of our special grace, certain
knowledge, and mere motion, have given and granted, and We do, by these Presents, for Us, our
Heirs and Successors, give and grant unto

Origins and History

*The newly purchased property at Boland Brook had a long,
interesting and fortunately, well-documented history.*

On November 22, 1836, King William IV (1765-1837) of England "by the grace of
GOD, of the United Kingdom of Great Britain and Ireland, <u>KING</u>, Defender of the
Faith, did grant to one James Rait, his heirs and assigns" of St. Andrews, New
Brunswick, Grant Number 959, composed of 1280 acres in the parishes of Addington
and Eldon in the county of Gloucester (now Restigouche County) (portion of original
grant shown above).

King William is one of the lesser-known English monarchs, since the only thing of
note for which he is known, other than granting these 1280 acres to James Rait, is the
support of various reform bills of the Parliament of 1832. On the advice of his Prime
Minister, the 2nd Earl Grey (presumably from whom all the tea comes), he supported
the Reform of 1833 abolishing colonial slavery, the reform of the poor laws in 1834 and
the Municipal Reform Act in 1835. He ruled from 1830 to 1837, succeeding his older
brother, George IV, and he himself was succeeded on the throne by his niece, Victoria.

His rule was short, but he was pretty much a good, reform-a-year man.

The original survey of the two tracts of land was done by one Joseph Hunter,
about whom little is known (Fig. 1, page 16). The grant specifically included riparian
rights, but no mention was made of mineral rights, which was to become a problem in
the distant future. The original Grant document remains in my possession.

Around the turn of the twentieth century the Boland Brook property changed
hands several times with Cyrus K. Fiske, an American who lived in Canada, becoming an owner and, subsequently, after his death, his daughter, Mrs. P. R. Inches, was
left the land. No records of this have been found, but on February 29, 1904,

Mrs. Inches sold both the Boland Brook and the Grog Brook properties to Mr. James F. Robertson, a prosperous merchant of Rothesay, New Brunswick, a suburb of St. John. James and his wife, Josephine, had the unabashed intention of enjoying some quality salmon fishing on the Upsalquitch. From here on, I will be following the history of only the upriver tract, the Boland Brook property, with 416 acres on the west

Figure 1: 1836 grant and survey by Joseph Hunter of Black family land holdings on the Upsalquitch River.

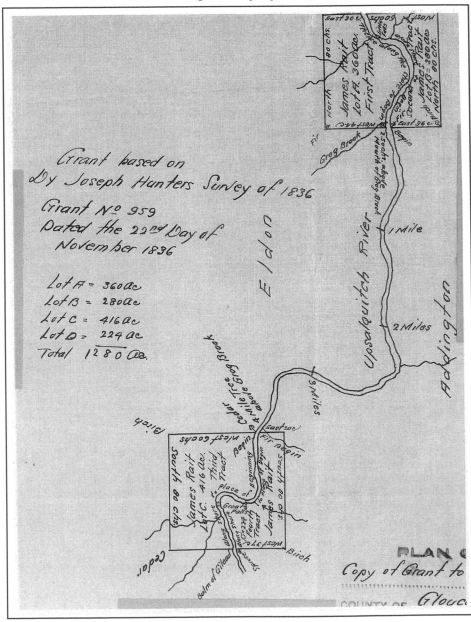

side (the Boland Brook side) of the river and 224 acres on the east side of the Upsalquitch River.

James traveled up river to his newly purchased land on a flat-bottomed scow, towed by a horse and rider no doubt, to supervise the cutting of trees for building his fishing camp. He chose an area downstream from the future Boland Brook campsite, an area overlooking a pool he christened *Josie's*, a productive pool, which still carries Josie's name today. Eleven buildings were constructed and he named the new camp, Camp Useppa, an Italian version of Josephine, after his second and current wife at the time, Josephine Hooper Robertson. Six guides were employed, four to guide the fishermen, one to cook and one to cure and smoke the salmon caught from the river. Josephine has said that her husband always took $600 in cash with him from Rothesay to pay the six guides for the month they spent each summer at Camp Useppa. This currency probably also covered any additional expenses, such as food and time the guides spent opening and closing the camp. James Robertson had leased the Boland Brook property for two years, before he bought it, and returned to the Upsalquitch for seventeen consecutive summers, with the exception of one year during World War I, when he gave the $1,000 it cost him annually to run the camp to the war effort.

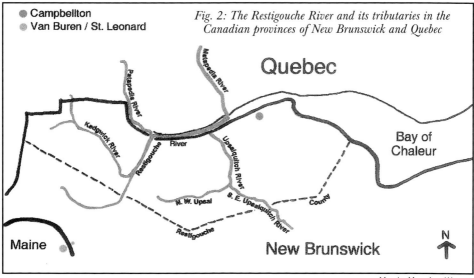

Fig. 2: The Restigouche River and its tributaries in the Canadian provinces of New Brunswick and Quebec

Map by Mary Ann Weems

So each summer, but one, the Robertsons left Rothesay in southern New Brunswick about 6:30 p.m. on the train, traveling north to reach Campbellton, New Brunswick, at 4:00 a.m. the next day. There in the Campbellton station they made tea with the aid of a "spirit lamp" (alcohol lamp) and ate sandwiches for their breakfast, before boarding at 7:00 a.m. another train, which stopped to let them off at the settlement of Upsalquitch at about 9:30 a.m. Their guides met them there, took them to the river, and on horses towed them up river in a scow or in two Gaspé boats or canoes tied side-by-side together. After arriving at Camp Useppa, the first order of the day was putting up the screens on the windows in the camp and setting up the rods, which were probably heavy, bamboo cane rods, eleven to fourteen feet in length, customary sporting gear in that era for battling salmon.

The Robertsons had many prominent people as their guests. The quality of the fishing was best described by Andrew Carnegie's brother-in-law, a Mr. Whiteman, who euphorically said, "At Skibo Castle, if one salmon is killed, the whole village turns out to see it, while here I have killed twenty five myself!" Skibo Castle was the Carnegie Estate in Scotland. The average daily catch at Useppa was eight salmon, usually weighing between ten to sixteen pounds. It is not known whether the grilse catch were recorded or included in these numbers. Grilse are Atlantic salmon, that have left the freshwater environment at two to three years of age, migrated for the first time to the ocean and are returning to spawn, after having spent only one winter in the sea. The size of grilse vary from river to river, usually weighing between three and seven pounds; they are strong fighters and in all appearance similar to the larger salmon, which have spent multiple winters in salt water.

Author playing a fish at Josie's Pool, circa 1970.

The Useppa camp record was a forty-five-pound salmon, a really huge fish, caught in 1915 by one of the Robertsons' guides, George Thomas. As far as I know, it still is a record for the Upsalquitch River. In 1950, two friends of mine, Fred VanPoznak and Lee Bartholomew, and I were camped for the night on the upper river at an area called Crooked Rapids, when an elderly, but still vigorous, George Thomas was poling his canoe up river and pulled it onto the gravel beach to join us for the night. Around the campfire and in our sleeping bags, we were entertained for several hours with stories of life on the river that seriously strained our powers of belief, even though we were young and impressionable. The story of the forty-five-pound salmon was true, as there is verification elsewhere of this extraordinary event. At this time I knew next to nothing about Boland Brook's history or I might have pressed George for even more information about the camp that was so important to me.

In 1919 the Boland Brook (Camp Useppa) property was sold again, this time to Mr. William A. Black of Halifax, Nova Scotia. He and his family, Watiqua Inc, owned it until September 17, 1936, when it was sold to my aunt, Miss Katharine deB. Parsons.

3

Building and Furnishing

*After leaving the Upsalquitch River in the second week of
August 1936, Katharine Parsons returned briefly in
the same month with some simple paper and pencil sketches
of various buildings and floor plans for the camp to be.*

She then staked out the locations of those buildings, using her own transit, the sophisticated instrument used by surveyors and engineers. Her transit remains in its wooden box on the top shelf of a Boland Brook closet; no other family member has ever learned how to use it. On her return to her New York apartment she intensified her work, using T-square and compass to fine-tune her drawings for the camp buildings, planning their location on the property and their relation to each other. Relationships between buildings were especially important to avoid losing multiple structures in the case of fire. In addition, she was calculating the cost of the camp construction and the future costs to operate it. There was never any question about what this new camp would be called; it was to be Boland Brook Camp. If you are beginning to realize that this was an unusual woman, you are right. She was an extraordinary woman, who was carefully planning her future summers with excitement, commitment and with just a little trepidation, as she contemplated her ownership of a fishing camp, a prime salmon-fishing location and a square mile of wilderness in a country other than her own.

Architect and friend, William E. Shepherd of New York City, was asked to draw up the detailed plans and specifications for a contractor to follow in the building of the camp. On his part, this was probably a kindness to a friend, since his professional services were much in demand for larger projects. His task was simplified, as there would be no electrical wiring, since there was no source of electricity and no elaborate heating diagrams were needed, as fireplaces were to be the sole source of heat in the buildings. D.W.

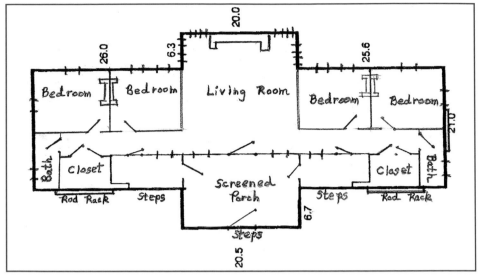

Fig. 3: Boland Brook Camp Lodge — Main Bldg. The screened porch faces the Upsalquitch River.

Stewart of Campbellton, New Brunswick, was selected as the contractor and Bill Robertson of Upsalquitch agreed to act as supervisor and liaison between the owner and the contractor. Most of all the arrangements were made without face-to-face discussion and Katharine had to rely on the advice and help of the few local people she had met.

The dirt road along the lower Upsalquitch ended five miles below Boland Brook, from that point on all building materials had to be loaded on a flat-bottomed scow and towed up river by a horse and rider, or, if the load were heavy, by two horses with the rider astride one of the two. A young horse could also be broken-in by working along-side a more seasoned horse. It was a three-hour trip by scow going up to the campsite and an hour and a half float on the way back with men and horses loaded on the scow. In this region scows were the customary method for hauling supplies or groups of people up the rivers. They were ten feet wide and approximately twenty-two feet long with a height of eighteen inches from water to the top of the gunnels. There was a stout post solidly fixed in the bow to which the hefty rope from the horse's harness could be wound. A bowman stood here to watch the rope and release it quickly, if the horse lost his footing, or with his spruce pole at the ready to fend off the bow from striking a rock just below the water's surface. In the stern, another man handled "the sweep," a long rudder hewn from a single tree, to provide help with steering and maintaining the scow's position near the bank. The bowman, the stern man and the horse worked as a team, slowly but steadily, pulling the scow and its contents up the river against the fast flow of the current. Larger scows were used in logging operations along the northern New Brunswick rivers to carry supplies for the loggers and to provide shelter. Tents were erected on the scows to house cots and sleeping bags and a stove for the cook. The scows' sturdy construction, shallow draft and minimal resistance to the flow of the river current, made them the ideal method for river travel.

As the camp sprang up, the carpenters at Boland Brook spent many nights in tents, as commuting from their homes miles away daily was impractical, but the discomfort of cold fall nights outdoors was probably offset by the absence of black flies and mosquitoes. When snows covered the ground, work had to be discontinued until the following spring.

The camp was built on a relatively flat area of several acres on the west side of the Upsalquitch River. On the upper end of this flat area, fast-flowing, gin-clear (vodka may be substituted, if you prefer), rock-bottomed Boland Brook served as a boundary, entering the river at a downstream angle to join the Camp Pool, which

Scow loaded with lumber on Camp Pool, 1938.

was situated directly in front of the sprouting camp buildings. The Camp Pool, which was called Boland Brook Pool on older maps, had the reputation of being one of the best salmon pools on the river. This was due to the cold brook water entering at the head of the pool, and also, in my opinion, to the annual, spring log drives down the brook that served to dig out the pool maintaining it at a five- to seven-foot depth.

Behind the location for the camp was a low ridge, a quarter of a mile beyond which was a large beaver pond and a surrounding swamp, the site of the future source of the camp water supply. There was a good thirty-foot differential between the pond and the camp, which would by gravity flow provide excellent water pressure. A water sample was sent off to a laboratory for testing and the subsequent report described the water as "moderately hard" and containing no coliform (intestinal) bacteria.

The decaying remains of several small log cabins were burned or removed. These were the remains of an old logging camp, since, sometime around 1925, two men named Borland and Duncan had formed a logging company and supposedly had their headquarters at Boland Brook. Logging was done by acquiring rights on provincial land and small pulp logs for eventual use as paper were floated down Boland Brook each spring, then floated down the Upsalquitch to its junction with the Restigouche River and from there down to the paper mill at Atholville, a village near Campbellton at the head of the Bay of Chaleur. I do not know what happened to Borland and Duncan, but the International Paper Company, the I.P., took up where they left off. Only one old building on the site was in good enough condition to be spared and it was actually moved about fifty feet from its original location for incorporation into "the Guide House" in the new camp.

The main building of Boland Brook Camp, built facing the river, but set back about two hundred feet from the bank, in case there might be springtime river flooding, had a central screened-in porch, which had a front door entry into the living room, where a large fireplace faced the door to the porch. Each of the two halls, which extended out at right angles from the living room, had two bedrooms opening off them and at the end of each hall was a bathroom with a flush toilet and a washbasin with a single spigot for cold water from the beaver pond. There was a small fireplace in each of the four bedrooms, since a cheery fire was the only source of heat on a cold morning or a damp, rainy day.

The next largest building was the combined dining room and kitchen. The kitchen had a large cast iron, wood-burning stove, on top of which a huge pot of hot water was always steaming. There was also a double sink, an icebox (not a refrigerator) and a

L. Parsons, Russell Murray, L. Parsons Jr., and Katharine deB. Parsons discuss one of the rod racks at the back of the main building, 1937.

dining alcove with a table and a bench on either side of it, where the camp staff would have their meals. Opening off the kitchen was a bedroom intended for one or two female staff. On the end of this building, closest to the main building, was a full bathroom with a toilet, an iron tub supported by four iron lion's paws and a sink with two spigots to accommodate cold water from the beaver pond and hot water heated by the kitchen stove on the other side of the wall. On this same end of the building there was also a dining room designed to comfortably seat six people, or as many as eight in a pinch.

Other buildings were the one-room guide house, an icehouse, a barn, and a combined wood shed and tool shed in another small building. The icehouse was a double-walled structure, with sloping roof and a single room, where ice from the river was stored and perishable foods could be kept. The barn contained two stalls for horses and another for the cow and her calf, plus storage areas for grain and hay. Behind the main building a root cellar and a fire box for smoking fish were dug out of the hillside. The root cellar had a wooden frame door, but was otherwise just a dirt cave. The smoking structure had a grill several feet above the fire pit on which the fish were placed for smoking and above the grill there was a tunnel through the ground, which led upward for several feet before it opened out on a flat spot on the hillside.

Lastly there was Steven's Cabin. The latter was a small, two-room cabin built on a low bank overlooking Boland Brook, named Steven's Cabin because one of its two rooms was to be occupied each summer by Katharine Parsons' chauffeur, who drove her from New York City to the Upsalquitch each summer and back to New York City at the summer's end. As did all visitors, Steven loved his time at Boland Brook Camp and seemed to thrive in the outdoor environment of the woods, doing every odd job that needed to be done around the camp, exploring the woods in his spare time and learning the art of poling a canoe. He would help pole guests up river, poling in the bow of the canoe with a guide poling in the stern. He was a large man, well over two hundred pounds, with white hair, glasses and a constant smile. I was a boy when I knew him and Steven was the only name for him I ever knew and, if someone were to speak his last name today, I am sure I would not recognize it. He suffered a stroke in his seven or eighth year at the camp while in the woods about half a mile away. With great difficulty he was brought out of the woods in a makeshift stretcher and taken down river to the hospital in Campbellton. He survived to return to his home in New York City, but was never able to drive again. Katharine Parsons assisted in getting him a job as a doorman in a Manhattan apartment building, but he was never able to return to his beloved Boland Brook. Steven has long since left us, but not his memory. His room in Steven's Cabin became my aunt's carpentry shop, but nowadays, since I am less adept than she with saw and chisel, it has been converted to my fly-tying and rod repair shop.

The larger camp buildings were built on concrete piers raising them a foot off the ground and were built almost entirely of spruce, which was readily available. There was no insulation as they were only to be occupied in summer, but the outside surfaces were weather proofed with Linseed oil, which was reapplied annually. The roofs were constructed in layers with wood, felt and asphalt slate shingles. The handsome fireplaces were made from smooth, colored stones brought up from the river. There were flagstones of granite, also obtained from the river, that were used to make a path from the main building to the dining room. On the front and one side of the main building, rod racks with protective overhangs were created. (See Fig. 3, page 20)

All furniture, with the exception of two wicker chairs and a sofa in the living room, was made by a Nova Scotia carpenter personally known to my aunt Katharine, who, in her precise way, had specified the dimensions of each piece, so that each would comfortably fit in its destined location in its destined room. The wicker items, as well as most of the other camp furnishings, came from Eaton's Department Store in Montreal.

Blankets were ordered from Hudson's Bay Company of Canada, and the official camp china was a fine set of English china. Kerosene lamps provided lighting after dark; a special variety, called Aladdin Lamps, ordered from L.L. Bean in Maine, were used in the living room, because their shape and soft light produced by incandescent wicks and large, white shades made them resemble electric lamps. Katharine Parsons kept notebooks in which the cost of every item from frying pans to nails used in the construction and furnishing of the camp was listed.

At Boland Brook Camp there was no central heating, no electricity and hot water in only one location, the bathroom off the kitchen, unless you included the large pot of hot water on the back of the stove. Not a deluxe or plush camp, but a comfortable hideaway with great ambiance, designed for the hard-core salmon fisherman. The word "hard-core" in the last sentence is probably redundant, since I cannot recall an Atlantic salmon fisherman who is not aggressively enthusiastic about this sport, if not hyperactively passionate about it.

Kitchen cabin with guide house in the rear, 1937.

CHAPTER

Moving In

*ince the Upsalquitch River valley had been timbered in the first
quarter of the twentieth century and burned by a devastating,
large forest fire that swept across northern New Brunswick in 1923,
the land around Boland Brook Camp was sparsely covered with
new-growth trees, most less than seven to eight feet in height.*

Healthy patches of spruce and Balm of Gilead trees were spared in some places along the river and along Boland Brook. The relatively barren landscape allowed deer and bear to be easily spotted on the hillsides. The open areas of ground afforded blueberries, which need ample sunlight, to grow in profusion on these same hillsides, making it possible to spot multiple black bear in the late summer getting their blueberry fix.

In the midst of this landscape, Boland Brook Camp had been completed, an isolated enclave in the wilderness and a handsome fishing camp, if ever there was one — a delight to any fisherman (and possible even a non-fisherman) fortunate enough to be invited to visit.

The contractor, D.W. Stewart, and Bill Robertson, the supervisor, had done great jobs. Katharine Parsons arrived at her new fishing camp, that neither she, nor her architect had ever seen during any phase of its construction, on June 19, 1937, with her good friend, Bunny Avery, who had been her companion on several enjoyable, but unsuccessful, previous salmon fishing excursions in Nova Scotia. She was delighted by what she found. It was a shame that the architect never would get to see it.

She recorded her feelings in the camp record as follows: "On Saturday, the 19th of June, 1937, we arrived at Boland Brook Camp for the first time since it was finished. It was an exciting moment, when we rounded the bend of the river at The Falls and saw our buildings. I was almost afraid to look, as I had pictured in my mind's eye exactly how I wanted them to appear. I was not disappointed. That day we worked like beavers, unpacking crates and boxes and by evening had the camp practically settled - furniture in place, china and kitchen utensils washed. We went down river for the week-end, moving in and officially opening the camp on Monday, June 21st."

Salmon had been seen jumping in The Camp Pool all through the weekend, so in the next days a few forays were made out onto the river and the first few entries made in the camp Fish Register, in which every fish caught at Boland Brook from the day the camp opened to today is recorded. The Fish Register is a large, leather and canvass-bound ledger, which always resided in the center of a long table in the living room. The area on the left of each page was for signatures; then the columns from left to right were for: "salmon or grilse", then the fish's "weight", then the "pool" in which the fish was caught, then the "fly" pattern and size, then the "time" of day and then a last column for "remarks". The last column could include comments about the height or condition of the river, the weather, whether the fish was kept or released, the length of the battle or anything that seemed special or unusual. Katharine, in beautiful, legible handwriting, recorded all the information except the name of the angler, who would sign his or her name to the left of the appropriate data. The signing of the Fish Register was almost a formal ceremony, held twice a day when all returned from the morning and evening fishing. Woe be the person who signed an illegible signature, no matter how proud of it the perpetrator might be, because it would be effaced with "White-Out" ink eraser, and the offender subjected to a lecture on penmanship, before a second try was allowed. There are additional pages in the Fish Register, which record the number of salmon and grilse taken in each pool during each month of the fishing season and totals for salmon and grilse taken each year. The records are accurate and painstakingly kept.

There is now a second volume of the Fish Register, but the valuable data on every salmon or grilse ever landed at the camp is available. The information has proven useful time and time again to individuals looking up their personal totals, for governmental and private groups doing river or regional studies and for articles written in papers or in magazines, not to mention looking for that right fly pattern that was so successful in high water last year in the Frying Pan Pool.

There is also a guest book signed by each guest at Boland Brook with the dates of their visits recorded and the length of Katharine Parsons' stay each summer. Another important camp record book is The Boland Brook Camp Chronicle, now in its third volume. The Chronicle was started by Wallace Turnbull and contains anything that anyone who has been at the camp, might wish to write. Some of it is thank you so much for material, but much of it records, in poetry and prose, happenings of note at camp and along the river, summaries of the year at camp, cartoons and newspaper clippings pertinent to salmon fishing in New Brunswick. Truly a priceless record of the years passed.

Another very important object in the new camp was the only telephone, the only direct connection with the outside world. In those days, telephones were used primarily for emergencies and critical information, rather than for entertainment, prestige, gossip or just to pass the time. On sober second thought, gossip should be removed from my list since the telephone has always been used for that. The Boland Brook telephone was on old-fashioned wooden, crank job, mounted outside the kitchen door, so that it could be used by anyone at any time of year, who might be going up or down the river. Cranking the handle vigorously raised Mrs. Murray in the settlement, who, if she were home, could throw a switch and connect you to the Campbellton operator. It was always difficult, at times impossible, to hear an attempt at a long-distance call, regardless of whether it was incoming or an outgoing call and the conversation could be heard all over the camp and, perhaps, by the fish in the river. The phone line was a single, large-diameter wire, about fifteen miles long, installed originally by the I.P. about one hundred yards back from the river. Each camp was responsible for keeping

their segment of the phone line functioning, which meant walking along it after thunderstorms and high winds to clear fallen branches or trees lying across the line. This problem increased as the years went by and as the burned-over forest regrew around the line.

On the line up river was a fire tower with a resident fire warden, the I.P. cookhouse, the fish wardens' camps at Reid's Gulch and Crooked Rapids and the fishing camps at The Forks, Two Brooks and Berry Brook. There was not much formal entertainment along the river, particularly for the solo fire warden, and anytime the phone rang, receivers were raised all along the line. A good joke was followed by laughter from multiple sources and it was not unusual to have advice offered by a third party to the two primary conversers, when a problem was being discussed, such as how to repair a leaking canoe. The call number to reach Boland Brook Camp was three long and three short rings, generated by turning a crank on one of the other phones along the line. A few years after 1937 a

Crank phone on the I.P. line and "phone book" used in the early years at Boland Brook camp.

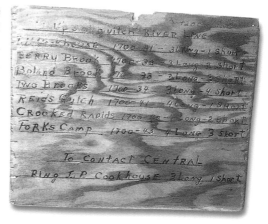

second, but similar, phone was installed in one hall of the main building and the "phone book" hung on the wall next to it. This consisted of a small, square piece of plywood with the various ring numbers for phones along the river burned into it. Although no longer used, the phone remains in place as a nostalgic reminder of by-gone days.

Boland Brook Camp had been built, had become inhabited and was now ready for the serious business of fishing for Atlantic salmon.

5

An Introduction

$\mathcal{N}$ow Katharine deB. Parsons had become the proud and original owner of Boland Brook Camp.

There is no question in my mind that Katharine Parsons had foresight, and perhaps courage, to purchase a remote square mile of New Brunswick forest, but as I have said, she was one of a kind, an unusual woman, who in this instance acted decisively, when she recognized opportunity was knocking on her door.

She was my father's only sibling, his younger sister, and a very austere and often intimidating personality, at least as far as my two sisters, Diana and Sally, and myself were concerned. The three of us called her "Allie" or "Aunt Allie" for reasons no one could ever recall, but I suspect my older sister, Sally, started it and the other two of us followed suit. My father and mother and Allie's closest friends called her "Kay" or "K.P."; everyone else called her "Miss Parsons". If any acquaintance, employee, tradesperson, doctor or lawyer called her otherwise, their relationship was terminated on the spot. I can remember when her banker encountered my father at a cocktail party and briefly mentioned some aspect of her finances to him. When my father mentioned the discussion to her, she called her banker immediately to say she was transferring her account to another bank, because she did not appreciate her personal business affairs being discussed at a social occasion, even when it was with her brother. Furthermore, she always insisted her name be spelled correctly, her first name with a " K" and two "a"s and her middle name with a small "de" and a large "B" and she believed no respectable woman would have her address printed on her checks, and certainly not her phone number. She made it plain that she had no use for the term "Ms." to the day she died in 1993.

Keeping all of this in mind, I was more than a little surprised and very excited, when my father, Livingston Parsons, informed me shortly after school had ended in the summer of 1937 that the two of us had been invited to go salmon fishing at Boland Brook. I had just barely reached my eleventh birthday and my previous fishing experience had been limited to catching "snappers" (baby blue fish) with a bamboo pole and a bobber in Long Island Sound and flipping out "sunnies" with even more rudimentary equipment from the Byram River, which was actually a brook, located down the long hill and across Riversville Road. This was in Greenwich, Connecticut, where I grew up. "Snapper" fishing was usually a family affair, fishing off a dock or jetty on an incoming tide with sandwiches and soft drinks available. Byram River, on the other hand, required that my good friend and next-door neigh-

bor, Stuart Lovejoy and I be outfitted with a long branch, some string, a bent pin and some bread crumbs. With this background, it certainly looked like I was soon to be over my head in the fishing arena. Perhaps, as a result of having read all of Ernest Thompson Seton's books, I informed Stuart Lovejoy

Ferguson's Turn Pool on the Upsalquitch River, 1939.

and my other friends that my father and I were going fishing in "the great north woods." Excitement and anticipation built and I felt reasonably secure that my father would provide any protection I might need from the elements, wild animals and even the somewhat formidable Aunt Allie.

The appointed day finally arrived, a Sunday afternoon, and mother drove us from Greenwich to the Stamford Connecticut railroad station for the several-hour train ride to Backbay Station in Boston. Dad and I were both outfitted in coats, ties and fedora hats, the male traveling garb of that time, as long-distance travel was not only less commonplace, but more of a formal occasion than it is today. We had dinner in a Boston hotel; I do not remember the name of the hotel, yet it was an occasion for my father and I to be dining together without my mother or my sisters in attendance. About nine o'clock that evening we boarded the Potato Land Express of the Bangor and Aroostock Railroad in Boston's North Station for the second leg of a long trip. After a restless night in a Pullman berth, we awoke in Aroostock County, Maine, where the train crawled through endless potato farms spread over the rolling Maine countryside with unnecessarily prolonged stops at one small hamlet after another, Mars Hill, Houlton, Presque Isle, Caribou and New Sweden, to the end of the line at Van Buren, Maine, on the St. John River, which was the Maine-New Brunswick border. A guide from Boland Brook Camp met us there with his car, which from appearances had provided faithful service for more than a few years.

Author, age 11, with two salmon, 1937.

After crossing the border into Canada, we had a quick lunch in the old three-story St. Cyr Hotel in St. Leonard, Van Buren's smaller counterpart on the Canadian side. After lunch we had eighty miles of dirt road to traverse through the towns of St. Quentin, Kedgwick and St. Jean Baptiste. These were small French Canadian towns dominated by large cathedral-type churches, which seemed unduly large for their small communities. However, what I remember most clearly, since automobiles did not offer air conditioning in 1937, was having to frantically roll up all the windows to prevent suffocation from billowing clouds of dust that arose when another car passed us and then rolling them down as soon as we had outdistanced the dust, so that we could breathe some moving air and avoid the stagnant heat of the closed-up vehicle. By the time we descended the long hill that was the approach to the Upsalquitch valley, Dad and I, still in our city clothes, were drenched in dust and sweat.

It was yet another eight miles of narrow dirt road along the river road to "the landing." This consisted of two ruts angled down the riverbank between the trees and bushes to a small rocky beach, where a second guide and a Gaspé boat awaited us. The road from St. Leonard to the Upsalquitch has long since been paved, as has the river road, but "the landing" today remains just as it was in 1937, two parallel ruts steeply angled down the riverbank. The clean, fresh smell of the woods and the river itself also remain unchanged. After two hours of driving, it was refreshing to be sliding up the clear, fast-flowing river in the ultimate of beautiful surroundings with the rhythmic and seemingly effortless poling of our guides. Excitement was generated by the gray shadows that occasionally drifted away from our boat, as we forged up river at a steady rate moving through beautiful pools with names like Wharf, Berry Brook, Slide, Limestone, Ferguson's Turn and Waden's Rock. After twenty-seven hours of travel, it was close to five o'clock with light rain starting to fall, when we arrived at

Boland Brook to be greeted by my Aunt Katharine, who was anxious to show us around her brand-new fishing camp.

Shortly after supper, around 7:00 p.m., Allan Murray, my assigned guide, and I headed down river to fish below The Falls, the largest rapids on the Upsalquitch River. My eyes were not too far above the gunnels of the canoe and the awesome waves were almost up to my eye level. "The Great North Woods" were exceeding my expectations. Allan, only seventeen years old, but an accomplished river man and guide, patiently struggled to teach me how to cast my inexpensive, L.L. Bean fishing rod, which seemed three times as long as me. It was raining cats and dogs and as I steadied myself repeatedly in the canoe before each new cast, the river seemed awfully deep, swift and uninviting. Besides, it seemed to be getting very cold and dark, so after two hours of unrewarded effort, we returned to camp, where, cold and shivering, I was subjected to having my clothes forcibly removed, as I was hung out to dry by the fire with a lot more fussing than I thought was really necessary. As soon as Aunt Katharine (Allie) was out of earshot, I have been told, I asked my father: "How early can we go out fishing tomorrow?" This may have been an early indication that I had been short-changed in the random mixing of chromosomes and genes from two normal parents.

The next day was clear and sunny as Allan and I once again headed down river to fish in Josie's Pool. On the second "drop" of the canoe at 9:05 a.m. an event occurred that forever changed my perspective on life. There was a monstrous boil on the river surface, where my size-6 Black Dose was swinging in the current, the Bean pole arced toward the stern of the canoe and my old William Mills reel began to screech like a loose wheel on a roller skate. Thirty minutes later a nine-pound salmon was on the beach and I am sure my hands were shaking and my heart pounding. The time allotted for the morning's fishing was far from over, but I insisted that Allan pole us up river to camp, so that everyone could see the magnificent salmon and hear the

Livy Parsons Jr. with L.L. Bean rod in hand while guide Allan Murray holds the author's first catch at Boland Brook, a 9-pound salmon caught at Josie's Pool, 1937.

Author with his father Livingston Parsons, 1938.

whole story from beginning to end. If you do not believe all of this, I can assure you that it is well documented in the Fish Register that rests on the long table in the Boland Brook Camp living room.

It was not long after this that I could identify by names every commonly used salmon wet fly (dry flies were not yet in vogue). I knew that the "killick" was the lead anchor dropped from the bow of the canoe to hold the canoe in the current. I knew you called a male salmon a "cock" and a female salmon a "hen". I knew that you "killed" a salmon; you did not catch a salmon (thank heavens this salmon-speak is disappearing). I also knew that salmon don't bite or swallow a salmon fly, they "take" a fly; and depending on a variety of weather, river and other cosmic conditions, salmon are either "taking" or "not taking" in the river. I knew you shouldn't call your rod a pole. I even knew the difference between a salmon and a grilse. I must have been a real pain in the neck in my crusade to learn everything I could about these amazing fish and how to catch them. Actually, like everyone else, I was wrong about grilse. It took many years before we realized that they are not small three- to six-pound salmon, but that they are salmon that have only spent a single winter in the sea before returning to spawn.

There is not much question that the morning in early July, 1937, when I caught that nine-pound salmon at Josie's Pool was the start of my addiction to the pursuit of *Salmo salar*. The bad news is that we salmon addicts stop at nothing to fuel our addiction, (in common with other addicts that are even more serious social problems); the good news is that, so far, no one has found a cure for our particular addiction. This whole, serious situation is, perhaps, best summarized by a quote from Bruce Hutchison's book, *The Unknown Country*, "I have never regarded the confirmed salmon fisherman with hostility, but only with a deep compassion. For this madness there is no cure."

C H A P T E R

6

Camp Operation

oland Brook Camp was, by necessity, and in almost every respect, self-sufficient in the early years.

 A guide went down river (five miles by canoe and eight more miles by car) only twice a week to pick up the mail at the post office in Allan and Lyda Murray's house in Robinsonville, which was a scattering of farms and houses, where the bridge on the main road, which was a dirt road, crossed the Upsalquitch River. Camp guests were picked up on Mondays coming from Van Buren and other guests might have been driven back to Van Buren that same Monday morning. At any rate, Monday account-ed for one of the two weekly trips down river. There was no market or grocery store in Robinsonville or the smaller settlement of Upsalquitch and every few weeks a trip to Campbellton, twenty-eight miles north, might be necessary.

   Aunt Katharine's head guide was Russell Murray of Robinsonville, a man who had spent all his life on or near the Upsalquitch River as a farmer, logger and guide. He was held in great respect by all as capable, honest, reliable, and hard working— a perfect choice to manage the camp. He was soft spoken, but garnered respect with his dry wit and few words. He had a wonderful way with animals, which openly treat-ed him with affection, while, with them, he was stingy with his praises and firm in his commands. Russell always brought a cow and her current calf to camp, so that we had butter, fresh cream and milk daily with little or no concern about such things as pasteurization, Tuberculosis or Brucellosis. Twice each day he milked the cow among his other duties. Butter was made from a hand-rotated separator, and each Sunday we had home-made ice cream made with ground-up ice and salt in an old-fashioned ice cream maker where the paddles were turned by hand. For our eggs and an occasion-al dinner, there was a chicken coop with fifteen to twenty resident hens, at least at the beginning of the summer, and a good-sized vegetable garden was planted in early to mid June, when it was calculated that the last frosty night was over. By July there were plenty of fresh vegetables available from the garden, including lettuce, carrots, beets, peas, green beans and Swiss chard. Vegetables were canned toward the end of each summer to provide a supply for the beginning of the next season until the garden was producing. Root vegetables were stored in the root cellar.

The icehouse was a one-room building also partly in the side of a hill, but it was constructed entirely of wood in two layers with about six inches of air between the two

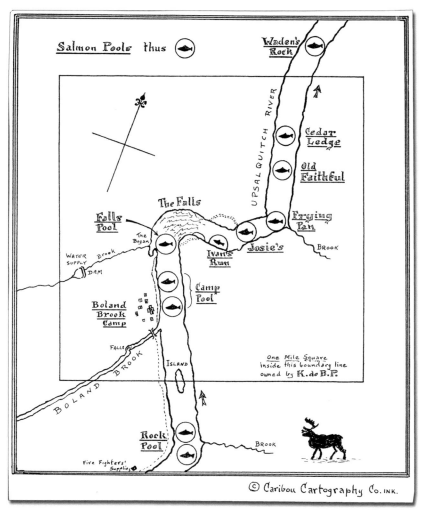

Fig. 4: Salmon pools on the Boland Brook water. Map by Wallace W. Turnbull.

layers. The doors, one in front to access the food storage shelves and a smaller one in back to access the ice, were similarly constructed, as was the peaked roof. Ice was cut from "the bogan", a small bay at the lower end of the Camp Pool, where there was little current. This was done in February, when the ice would be cut in large blocks, sixteen to eighteen inches thick, and hauled on a wooden sled up from the river to the icehouse, where they were covered with sawdust. The ice would last until the following fall, keeping the temperature in the icehouse at about forty-five degrees Fahrenheit, providing the door was not left open. The icehouse, our only source of refrigeration, was the repository for recently caught salmon, of which we always had an ample supply, since fish were plentiful enough to warrant a limit of twenty fish kept a week. At that time catch-and-release was not even on the horizon and would have been considered an unnecessary, if not a ridiculous, concept and explains why there are several photos in this book of anglers holding large salmon out of the water. The salmon were placed on the ice under the sawdust and cleaned only before being eaten. I think we ate salmon almost once a day in a great variety of culinary expressions, all of them good.

When it came to heat, our only sources of warmth were the fireplaces in the living room and bedrooms of the main building and in the dining room. Wood was cut each fall for the fireplaces, usually in October, when the flying insects had disappeared from the woods. To be sure the wood was dry, it would not be used in the summer following the fall when it had been cut, but two summers after cutting. Maple provided hard wood and cedar was used for kindling. The guides would build tiered fires in the bedrooms, four tiers in all, of thin strips of dry cedar. Anglers could jump out of bed on cold mornings, quickly light the cedar fires, jump back in bed and enjoy ten minutes of explosive crackling in the fireplace and flickering lights illuminating the walls, before getting up to dress in a now-warm room. There was an iron sheepherder's stove in the guide house to provide warmth there and the large, iron wood-stove did the job in the kitchen.

Cold water for the camp came through a long pipe from the beaver pond in the flat area up the hill about a quarter of a mile behind the camp. As mentioned earlier, light came from kerosene lamps at night when we needed it, supplemented by battery-operated flashlights and lamps.

Allie had room for up to five guests at Boland Brook, but really only enough water to accommodate fishing for two canoes, each with a guide and two anglers, one fishing the upper water and one fishing the lower water. Almost all fishing was done from canoes, since it was difficult to cover the water in most pools well with our flies from the shore, because of steep banks, bushes and fast current. Late in the summer, lower water provided exceptions. The upper water consisted of the Camp Pool and the head of The Falls. The lower water below The Falls consisted of Ivan's Run, Josie's, the Frying Pan, Old Faithful and Cedar Ledge (see illustration on pg. 34). The Falls are the major rapids on the Upsalquitch River, about one hundred yards long and intimidating in high water, a major test for guides poling their canoes up the river. Outboard motors had not yet entered the picture. It was not uncommon for someone unfamiliar with The Falls to overturn their canoe or smash it on the rocks in their descent of the rapids. This became more frequent in the 1980's and thereafter, as recreational canoeing became more popular in New Brunswick. Axes, cooking gear, cameras and the like were often found several hundred yards below The Falls at a later date. One summer in the late1990's canoeists lost their outboard motor in The Falls, returning the next weekend with a grappling hook and eventually retrieving their motor from the twenty-five-foot hole at the lower end of the rapids.

It was rusted and full of sand. In 2002, two government officials gave up on trying to run their canoe and outboard motor up through The Falls. I am not sure, but I think I saw a suspicion of a smirk on my guide's face on that occasion.

The Camp Pool, with Boland Brook entering at its head, was the most consistent fish producer and, if a salmon was not hooked on a specific drop, a rise or a prick could be anticipated by covering the water again with another fly, before dropping the canoe down. Salmon have never held at the foot of The Falls, a deep, ideal-appearing holding area, but always rest at the head of The Falls on a rock ledge in about eight to ten feet of relatively fast moving water, where they are usually visible through the slick surface and are frequently disposed to playing with a dry fly. It is the one place where a fisherman's nerves and reactions are severely tested by seeing every fraction of a second during a "take", when a salmon slides up or slashes up from the bottom. Most all of the time salmon hooked at the head of The Falls will head up stream, but every now and then a big and uncontrollable salmon will head down river through The Falls. On these occasions tension mounts and a rapid response has to be coordinated. If anglers and guide had gone ashore to play the fish, all had to quickly get back in the canoe for pursuit and the guide had to guide the canoe backwards through the channel between the rocks down through The Falls, braking the canoe's downstream progress with his pole, so that the fisherman could keep a semblance of a tight line. The chances of reaching the gravel beach at the foot of The Falls with the fish still on the line are about fifty-fifty. The leader or line will be cut on the rocks or caught around them about half the time, no matter what maneuvers are undertaken. If a salmon is landed that has gone down The Falls, it will leave all a little shaky and be considered a special victory. Our younger son, David, at age thirteen, hooked his first salmon at the head of The Falls and down through the rapids it went. An hour later a tired young man had a 7 1/2-pound salmon in the net. The excitement reached such high levels that at one point Dad had to take the rod for a few minutes while the stressed angler had to make a brief visit to the bushes along the bank. In years past, I can think of at least two graphite rods that were broken during trips through The Falls.

The downriver pools, with the exception of Josie's, are small, with two to three drops each. When fishing from a canoe, a "drop" is the area of a pool that can be covered by the angler/caster (livy's choice). He begins casting a short line, then gradually extends his casts to the longest comfortable distance. The guide then pulls up the killick, allows the canoe to slide down with the current to where the last casts had reached, drops the killick, anchoring the canoe at a new "drop", where the water has not yet seen a fly. The Upsalquitch, half the size of its mother Restigouche River, is such a beautiful river, usually gin clear, fast flowing over a gravel and rock bottom, as it weaves its way between steep, forested hillsides, that I am hard pressed to name my favorite pool, but I lean toward Josie's, the site of my initial triumph.

Ivan Firth, a beautiful caster, always guided Allie. I usually fished in the same canoe with them, seated behind them when we were anchored, since it was there that Allie thought she was safest and where I could do the least amount of damage with my wandering fly. Allie's standard fishing outfit was jodhpurs (English riding britches), below-knee rubber boots (Wellies), a checkered shirt, often a tie and a pith helmet to top it off. She wore the latter, even if I was not in the canoe. Russell Murray always guided my father and my mother, when she was with us. The third guide was Allan Murray, with whom I could identify, as he was about six years my senior and always in the mood for a prank or some fun. He was a relative of Russell, but not his son. It seemed that all the people in the settlements of Robinsonville and Upsalquitch were Murrays, Firths, MacDougals, Manns or Thomases, good people of Scottish ancestry.

My father knew Jack Pratt of New York City, who had a lease on thirty three miles of river above Boland Brook Camp, thirteen miles on the main Upsalquitch and ten miles on each of the Northwest and the Southeast branches. A word-of-mouth agreement was negotiated by my father, whereby Boland Brook could fish Rock Pool, a long, long pool just above the island that marked the upper end of the Boland Brook property. This allowed us to fish three canoes with all three guides on the river, rotating between the upper water, the lower water and Rock Pool. In the late 1940s, Allan Murray left to work full time as a scaler for the International Paper Company, but his wife, Lyda, still remained our postmistress in Robinsonville. Jim Murray, who was Russell Murray's son, replaced Allan.

The only member of the camp staff you haven't met is Mrs. Steeves, our English-born cook, who with her round, crinkled, white cap always on her head, fed us all with wondrous recipes for salmon from the icehouse and turned out souffles and other culinary miracles on the big wood stove, which was in operation twenty-four hours a day in the small, hot (sometimes too hot) kitchen. In addition, all laundry was boiled and washed on the wood stove.

We always had a dog of some variety, but always of dubious heritage and appearance. Gentle, the cow, and her calf had a two-acre, barbed wire, fenced pasture in which to graze. Gentle would break ranks about once a summer and we would get a phone call that she was down in the set-

Ivan Firth, Aunt Katharine's fishing guide, holds a nice salmon, circa 1950.

tlement, which required that Russell bring her back on the scow and repair the barbed wire fence. The two horses, Fly, a large, black mare, and Dusty, her daughter, had free roam of the camp, but were always on call to tow the scow. The horses were good-natured, presenting no threat to anyone, with the possible exception of the need to take a flashlight, if we were to walk around outside after dark. The entire staff did what needed to be done; guiding was only part of the guides' work and Boland Brook Camp's total isolation precluded any of the staff from going down river to their homes and families in the settlement, except on an occasional Saturday night after the day's fishing was complete.

CHAPTER
7

The Schedule

The early, original camp schedule remains intact to this day.
At exactly 7:00 a.m. every morning, except Sunday,
we awoke to the slamming of outside doors and loud clanks,
as the guides deposited cast-iron milk cans of hot water,
heated on Mrs. Steeves' stove, outside each bedroom door.

Two cans were placed outside the door, if the room had two occupants. On Sunday mornings, when there was no fishing, we had the luxury of not being awakened until 7:30 a.m. Since there was no hot water to be had anywhere but in the kitchen and the bathroom in the same building, it was a distinct pleasure to have hot water on a cold morning to splash on our hands and faces and to use for shaving, that is if you were old enough to shave. I remember one night I conceived a fiendish plan and concealed half a dozen small trout from the river in a pail under my bed. I was awake early, so that as soon as the guides came in with the hot water cans and left, starting with Aunt Allie, I quickly poured out the hot water from each can, replacing it with cold water and a small, live trout. I moved quietly and fast as lightning, remaining undetected and executed the plan to perfection. Back in my own bed, the ensuing uproar up and down the hall was a great reward for my efforts, but it quickly resulted in my being grounded for the morning's fishing, a very severe and totally unreasonable penalty.

Breakfast was at 7:30 a.m. and we were usually headed in our canoes to our assigned water by 8:15 or 8:30 a.m. I could never understand how long it took grown-ups to eat breakfast and do whatever they did after breakfast each morning, when there were salmon waiting to be caught in the river. The morning's fishing concluded no later than 11:45 a.m., since the staff ate lunch at noon and it was a criminal offense to be even a few minutes late getting back to camp, the only valid excuse for violation being that you were playing a fish and naturally did not want to break it off if it were time to return. The downriver boat had to calculate the time for the sports to walk up two trails, one around rapids at the head of Josie's and one around The Falls, while the guide poled the empty canoe up the two sets of rapids. The sports had their cocktail hour from noon to 1:15 p.m. (cocktail hour is an oxymoron, since it always takes longer), when we ate what local people call dinner, actually the big meal of our day. The afternoons were spent walking, tying a salmon fly or two, occasionally taking a swim in the chilly river, but mostly in reading and snoozing, which had a direct connection with cocktail hour and the hefty midday meal. A favorite activity of mine was riding bareback on Fly, with whom I had a good relationship. She was a very large mare and the only time she did me dirt was the day she stepped on my bare foot, leaving a painful, red "U" for several weeks. I was never dumped in the river or run under the clothes line. Supper, a lighter meal, was at 5:30 p.m., so all could be on the river until dark. Allie planned that all drinking be done after fishing hours and not before, to diminish the chances of someone losing their balance in a tippy canoe on the fast-moving river. It was a rule rigidly enforced, as was the custom with all her rules. It was a wise rule, which is still followed today.

Livy Parsons Jr. on Fly, with kitchen cabin and guide house in the background.

After returning to camp in the evening, the grown-ups would have a nightcap, or two, and gather around the fire for the usual hyperboles and prevarications about the day's fishing, an activity well known to all of you. Although it was frowned upon by my aunt, (as she did on almost everything I thought was fun at that age), my favorite evening entertainment was to slip over to the guide house (forbidden ground for grown-ups) to hear Allan Murray play the harmonica, while Russell Murray did an agile clog dance, the likes of which I had never previously encountered. This would be followed by singing with harmonica accompaniment. There may be a few readers who remember the creaking door and the ominous voice murmuring, "Who knows what evil lurks in the minds of men? Only 'The Shadow' knows." I had my costume and amused myself by tapping on windows and leering in at anyone who would take notice and feign horror.

The only variation from the camp routine was on Sundays with wake-up and breakfast a half hour later and no salmon fishing. To the best of my memory, this was not a provincial law, but a custom, or gentleman's agreement, that was universally respected by fishermen all along the river to "rest the pools". Sunday had to be endured, and sometimes I thought Monday would never come.

When the camp was built there were two flagpoles directly in front of the main building, easily seen from the river. Facing the camp, the Union Jack was flown on the left and the American flag on the right. The flagpole on the left flew the Union Jack, because of our staff's strong feeling for the United Kingdom and for their Scottish heritage. When our second camp manager, Jim Murray, a war veteran, died in 1991, he wanted the Union Jack draped over his coffin, but the mortuary refused to do it, because it was against the law. Political correctness was alive and well in Canada and a man could not even have a simple last wish respected. At some time later, in more recent years, the Maple Leaf became the official Canadian flag and a third flagpole was raised. Again, facing the camp, the American flag was flown on the right, the Maple Leaf in the middle and the flag of the Province of New Brunswick on the left. The flags were not flown every day, but on Saturdays, Sundays, holidays and whenever new arrivals were expected. Allie always did the raising and lowering herself. This was a serious business.

Allie could have been accused of being too rigid in directing the camp, but it must be remembered that it was unusual for a woman to be running a salmon fishing camp and those who worked for her and dealt with her needed to know what to expect and that she could be relied upon to keep her word. Even early on, Boland Brook Camp was known to be a good place to work.

There is so much to recall, but it is surprising how much remains clear in my mind of these wonderful boyhood days.

World War II, The Cannery

*orld War II came during the earlier years
of Boland Brook Camp, starting in
the summer of 1941.*

It wasn't until 1944 that the idea of contributing in an unusual way to the war effort was conceived. In 1944 and 1945, fishing went on as usual, but what was unusual was the operation of our cannery.

This new activity was heavily researched by Allie, then, quickly put into operation as a small means by which Boland Brook could support the war effort. Salmon were still plentiful, and since all of the salmon and most of the grilse were killed, there was always an ample supply for eating at the camp and for the guides' families and our friends down river in the settlement. In fact, when guests left camp, we usually sent a wooden box filled with cracked ice from the icehouse and several salmon home with them. The box went through customs easily at Van Buren and was loaded in the baggage car of the same train on which the homeward-bound fishermen were boarding. If the fish were headed for New York City, Connecticut or New Jersey, the Bangor and Aroostock Railway would open the wooden boxes in Boston, repack them with ice at no charge and send them on their way.

Now, let's get back to the cannery! Since most afternoons at Boland Brook were free for relaxation between morning and evening fishing, we spent most of those afternoons canning. Grosses of specially-lined cans were ordered and Steven's (the former chauffeur's) cabin was selected as headquarters for the operation. Freshly-caught salmon were cleaned in Boland Brook and taken to the kitchen, where they were cut in cross sections; about five of which sections could be fitted, with the addition of a teaspoonful of salt, into the specially-lined tin cans. Then the can tops were crimped on, solidly sealing them, with a device that looked not unlike some modern, hand-held can opener. This device held the can firmly, while a lever secured the top and then a hand-operated crank rotated the can as the edge was sealed. The operation progressed from the brook to the kitchen to the tool shed, where the actual canning was done. Next action was moved to the beach by the Camp Pool. The guides, after their lunch, would get a roaring fire going on the beach, cover the red-hot coals with an iron grate and place a fifty-gallon drum on top of the grate. This was filled half way up with water and brought to an enthusiastic boil, at which time the sealed cans of salmon would be brought from the tool shed in a wheelbarrow, then lowered into the boiling water, where they would remain for one hour. At the end of an hour, the cans would be removed from the drum with the shovel. At this time both ends of the cans would be bulging outward, but as they cooled, the ends would snap back in to their normal position. Any can whose ends did not snap back in were discarded, as this identified a leak. The "keepers" were taken to Steven's cabin on the wheelbarrow.

The next afternoon the process would continue in Steven's cabin on a workbench, where each can of salmon would have a wrap-around label attached with "Boland Brook Camp, Atlantic Salmon" and the date inscribed upon it. Eight cans were wrapped in heavy, brown paper as one package and tied in a strong net of twine, They were then addressed to different Canadian and United States regiments serving in the European Theater, the addresses having been obtained from the respective War Offices. The salmon was then ready to be mailed at the post office on the next trip down river.

Head guide Russell Murray boiling cans of fresh Boland Brook salmon, 1944.

Occasionally "thank you messages" arrived months later from appreciative servicemen in and near the front lines, a reward we all felt was worth more than the effort and expense involved in the endeavor. We gained satisfaction in learning that not all the salmon had been picked off by those who handled it during the long route between the Upsalquitch River and the intended recipients. For many years after the war, canning continued on a lesser scale, so guests could take salmon home to enjoy before returning to camp the next summer. The canned salmon was preserved indefinitely, and I can assure you it was delicious, hot, cold, or with more complicated culinary manipulation. Eventually canning came to a halt, because the source of the specially-treated cans went out of business and we could not find a substitute supplier. Probably government officials would now declare such canning activity illegal and our lawyer friends would inundate us with dire warnings, that we would be subjecting ourselves to all sorts of liability claims for endangering the lives of others.

9

The 1950s and the 1960s

*Below the Boland Brook water was the Berry Brook lease,
three miles leased, among others, by Messrs. Wilcox,
Shippee, Bryne and Fraser, who stayed in a cabin
on the hillside above the Berry Brook pool.*

Dana Lamb was also an annual visitor to Berry Brook and is remembered for his look-out tree, where a perch was built, from which he could observe the river, sketch and take notes for his writing. As I grew older I became increasingly aware of the extraordinary talent of this fine sportsman and have collected most of his publications for my library. Further down river was a stretch leased by Crosby and Sweet, but I do not recall ever meeting either of these two men and always sort of felt, when I heard their names mentioned by my aunt or my parents, that they were talking about a vaudeville act. Senator Sewell of Maine had a lease at Milbrook Farm near the river mouth in Robinsonville.

It was not much different with the upriver crowd. The John Pratt family from New York City leased thirty three miles of river above Boland Brook Camp, thirteen miles on the main river and ten miles up each of the two branches, the Southeast Upsalquitch and the Northwest Upsalquitch. The Pratts had a lovely camp at Two Brooks about five miles above Boland Brook and a decaying cabin at The Forks, where the two branches joined the main river. There were no roads anywhere along the upper river then and fishermen were poled up river in canoes by their guides to reach Two Brooks or The Forks, one day to reach the former and a second day to reach the latter. I remember members of the Pratt family passing our camp, as they went from the landing up river to their camps or down river on return, mainly Pratt daughters and their husbands, the Nitzis, Wilmerdings and Thayers.

In June of 1950, I graduated from Columbia University's College of Physicians and Surgeons and made plans with two of my co-graduates, Dr. Fred VanPoznak from New Jersey and Dr. Lee Bartholomew from Michigan (trout fishermen who had never fished for salmon) to head to Boland Brook on June 15, a week before Allie was due to arrive at camp. With permission, of course, we used Boland Brook canoes and guides. My plan was to go as far up the Northwest Upsalquitch as we could and fish our way down. This would be in remote, back country, accessible only by traveling on the river, as we were to do. I had written to Jack Pratt, who had kindly given us permission to fish in the twenty-three miles of his leased water that we would pass through. The three of us were due to start our internships on July 1st, and we were excited

Left to right: Lee Bartholomew, M.D.; Fred Van Poznak, M.D.; and Livy Parsons, M.D.; in June of 1950, just three weeks after obtaining their credentials.

about ten days of fishing and relaxation on a beautiful, New Brunswick salmon river. We took two canoes, poles, paddles, sleeping bags, provisions, and a small tent. We had a hunting rifle and I had a non-resident bear license (shown on page 45), good for four bears! Wow! What a deal! Since bears were always seen along the river, it seemed like bear hunting would be an extra added attraction we could all get enjoy. The four bears allowed us were four times as many as we saw on the whole expedition. Jim and Allan Murray would be our guides.

Every day of the trip involved excitement, new experiences, minor crises and near disasters, but I will touch only on a few of the highlights. The first night out of Boland Brook we poled all day to reach Crooked Rapids, where there was a one-room warden's cabin occupied by the warden, Billy Marshall. Billy was something of a legend in the area, a bachelor not well known for his association with soap and water or for stylish clothing. His cabin was dark and gloomy and we were not sure whether the strong assault on our sense of smell was due to Billy or his cabin; it was probably a combination of both. It was also rumored that he was overly fond of alcoholic beverages. In winter, Billy hibernated in a small hut in Robinsonville, making an appearance in the open air about once a month to purchase some food staples and presumably to replenish his supply of adult beverages. It was rumored that one winter he was found in serious condition in his sleeping bag with an empty bottle of saddle oil beside him, perhaps mistaken for other liquid nourishment. At any rate Billy cordially invited us in and, since at that point we decided that, if we were to accept, it would most likely be like sharing a den with a grizzly bear, we politely declined and elected to set up camp on the gravel beach along the river.

Supper was cooked over an open fire and Allan had pulled out his harmonica for a song or two before we crawled into our sleeping bags, when we were joined by another well-known river personality, George Thomas, a well-seasoned river guide who was also on his way up river. Realizing he had three city slickers in close range as a captive audience, he regaled us far into the night with stories of logjams, bears and mysterious drownings. Jim and Allan later told us most of the stories, though embellished, were probably true.

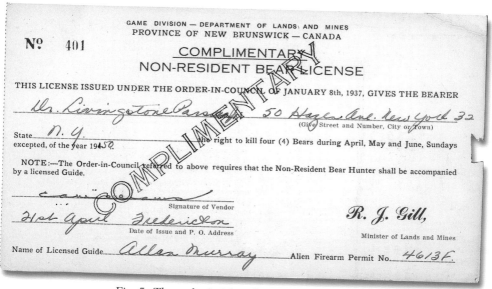

Fig. 5: The author's 4-bear license obtained in 1950.

The next morning, after an early start, we reached the cabin at The Forks at about 10:15 a.m. to find it inhabited by Herb Mann, a guide, and Arthur Bartlett, a cook. They insisted we have a snack before pushing on, producing coffee and four large pies, which they expected we would consume in their entirety. Allan whispered in my ear that Arthur was used to cooking in the lumber camps for loggers to explain the magnitude of the snack. While we were looking around among some old books and papers scattered seemingly at random around the cabin, I came across a small notebook with notes by George La Branche about dry-fly fishing for salmon. Ed Hewitt and LaBranche fished at The Forks and it was there that they gained much of the knowledge imparted in their classic books: *Secrets of the Salmon* (Hewitt, Charles Scribner Sons, 1922) and *The Dry Fly in Fast Water* (LaBranche, Charles Scribners Sons, 1914). Hewitt in his book mentions Ambrose Monell, saying "we have fished a number of seasons together in the Upsalquitch and tried many experiments." Speaking of LaBranches' book, the publisher says, "the book reflects original and outstanding contributions to the new sport of dry-fly fishing for Atlantic salmon, which was developed on Colonel Monell's water on the Upsalquitch." In those days there were numerous salmon on which to conduct their experiments.

On the next two days we were plagued by rain, but we took refuge in an old, decaying warden's shack at Nine Mile Pool on the Northwest. Actually, it was the shack that was decaying, not the warden that was decaying; there was no sign of a warden. Eventually we reached twenty-two miles up the Northwest, before starting our thirty-five mile trip back to Boland Brook. Fred lost a salmon at Nine Mile Pool, I lost one at Seven Mile, Fred lost one at Upper Promontory, Lee lost one at Humbug and I lost our fifth salmon in Caribou. We thought we were snake bitten and would never actually land a fresh-run Atlantic salmon. Lee finally did the trick, landing the only salmon of the trip one half mile above Boland Brook, to which we returned on the afternoon of June 21. Actually, it was still early in the season for very many fish to be in the river·

That last afternoon, several canoes passed us going up river to Two Brooks, the Jackson family, I believe. The camp records at Two Brooks has an entry, I am told, for June twenty-first, 1950: "About two miles above Boland Brook we saw two boatloads of grumous, disheveled, rain bedraggled, sinister appearing ruffians, bristling with whiskers and guns." Surprisingly, we were in the described area, but our party saw no such individuals. That trip was a wonderful experience and we still reminisce about it with laughter.

During the drive from New York City to the Upsalquitch that June we heard on the radio that the U.S. had become engaged in the Korean conflict on behalf of the United Nations. Within the next three years, the lives of all we three would be affected: Lee Bartholomew joined the Navy V-12 program, Fred VanPoznak became a Battalion Surgeon for the First Marine Division and was cited for valor under fire. I spent six months in the Prisoner of War Command in Korea and then served as Chief of Surgery at the 48th MASH. Since age eleven, I have only missed fishing at Boland Brook Camp in three years, the two years I was in the army and my first year in private, solo practice in Albuquerque, New Mexico.

People

*Coming from Albuquerque for my week or two at
Boland Brook Camp, I was often tired and,
perhaps, a bit frazzled by the long days and nights
and unending stress of a busy surgical practice.*

But when I would get in the bow of the canoe at the Upsalquitch landing, I would light my pipe, as we started up river, lean back, enjoying the sights, sounds and smells, slowly unwinding, enjoying everything as much as I did as a boy. The first few days in Camp I would crash after lunch, and in spite of a good night's sleep, would sleep the afternoon away. About two days of this and my tank would be full again.

Boland Brook Camp was always a happy place, a place to relax, where life was at a slower place, the surroundings were beautiful and there was the constant excitement of the fishing. The camp crew was always a happy one, and everyone always enjoyed living and working together. We looked forward to seeing our great staff every summer.

Mrs. Steeves with her frilly hat, was succeeded as our cook by Jean Ryan of Tidehead, a suburb of Campbellton; she continued the great New Brunswick style of cooking, complementing our frequent offerings of fresh salmon with souffles, Indian pudding, apple crisp, rice pudding, delicious pies, wild strawberry shortcake, cornbread, and my favorite, pineapple upside down cake.

Our three guides all had pleasant dispositions, dry senses of humor (for which guides are known), admirable skills in handling the canoes on the river, extensive knowledge about the fishing and were great company during the many hours a day spent on the river. Russell Murray was head guide and also the camp manager, but he was never called that, although his wisdom, understanding of all aspects of the camp, knowledge of

Russell Murray (l) and Livingston Parsons, 1938.

life along the river and unflappable manner, would have qualified him for the title. Ivan Firth, Allie's fishing guide, was the best caster and fisherman and the third guide was Allan Murray, a willing partner in most of my carefully concealed pranks of younger days. Russell always stayed at camp, because he was needed to milk the cow, feed the chickens and keep the farm going, but one of the two guides was allowed to go down river every third Saturday night, after the fishing was over, returning early Monday morning. There was no Sunday fishing. One Monday morning Ivan returned a little under the weather and with alcohol on his breath. My father and I were shocked, but not too surprised, when Allie told him unequivocally his employment had ended, to remove his belongings from the guide house and that he would be taken down river to his home immediately.

Alcohol consumption, or evidence of it, was forbidden to the camp staff. With Allie there was no second chance. Arbitration was not her long suit. Allie was sometimes alone at Boland Brook and she was the only woman in the area managing a fishing camp, so she had felt it necessary from the start to establish that she meant business. It always amazed me how fast important news seem to get up and down the river among the sparse outposts. Ivan's story was known everywhere within hours.

Jim Murray, Russell's son, a man only six months in age removed from myself, replaced Ivan. He became a close, lifelong friend. Jim was one of our guides in that famous expedition up the Northwest in 1950. He was a big man, strong as an ox, occasionally a little stubborn, a tireless and enthusiastic fisherman, particularly when it came to working a dry fly; he had all his father's attributes, filling his father's shoes well, providing competent management and guiding skills for many years. Jim died at Boland Brook Camp an August night in the 1991 as a relatively young man. We had emergency medical equipment, but he expired in the canoe, as we were taking him down river to the hospital. Travel on the river at night was always deemed dangerous, because of inability to see the rocks, but this time we had no choice. Wayne Borden was at the stern working the outboard motor, I was in the bow with a battery torch and Jim's wife, Peggy, was at hs side, as he was taken down river. We all lost a great friend that dark night. That very morning he had hooked a 26-pound salmon on a dry fly at The Falls, a fish that my wife landed for the camp record. It was the way Jim would have wanted to spend his last day. We still miss his sly smile and his reply of "not too bad" to an inquiry of how he was each morning. Peggy Murray worked at Boland Brook for forty-five years, doing just about everything –– cleaning, waiting on the table, doing the laundry and anything else that needed to be done that the men could not or would not do. She was an invaluable, loyal member of the team.

Russell always guided my parents, Sarah and Livingston Parsons, when they were at Boland Brook. Dad was a New York banker, who worked for the Manufacturer's Hanover Bank, which eventually became The Hanover Bank. He was born in New York City, went to Harvard and lived in New York City for many years before moving to Greenwich, Connecticut. He enjoyed hunting and fishing and was a quiet man with the wry Parsons sense of humor. He was certainly a good father, but not lavish with his praises. When my father was fishing alone at Boland Brook, he and Russell worked rapidly through their assigned water, usually being the first to return to camp and usually with one or more fish. The limit in the earlier years was twenty fish a week and, more often than not, my father caught his limit. He was discouraged, if he didn't. Neither man said much when they fished together, but both had a common bond in overseas service in the army in World War I, Russell in the renowned Black Watch regiment and my father in the Rainbow Division, in combat at Chateau Thierry and Belleau Wood in the Argonne Forest of France. Both men were wounded in action. My father's commanding officer was a young Col. Douglas MacArthur, who later achieved both fame and notoriety.

Russell Murray, the consummate river man, died in 1962. With his known love of animals, it seemed ironic that his death resulted from complications of a badly fractured arm after an accident with Bud, one of his beloved horses. Without his presence, things at Boland Brook Camp changed. The camp became less self-sufficient. We had to give up the cow, the calf, the chickens and even the two horses, Fly and Dusty, who pulled our scow up river from the settlement with supplies and arriving fishermen. About this time, outboard motors appeared on the river, replacing poling as the means of upriver travel. Progress? I suppose so. The initial fears that outboards would be damaging to the fishing proved to be unfounded; only the tranquility of the peaceful river suffered. We didn't need the horses. We didn't need the scow.

Allan Murray (l) and Livingston Parsons, 1941.

My mother would accompany my father, if the weather were good, reading and writing poetry, when she was not fishing. She was not the hard-core fisherman that we men were. Her fishing garb usually included rolled-up blue jeans and a jaunty, visored bonnet, for which she was nicknamed Daisy Mae. Examples of her poetry follow. I will preface the following excerpts from her poem, Choice, with a statement that in the early days, what we now call the "jet set", were often referred to in New York City as "Café Society", and these unfortunates frequented popular and peculiar night spots, such as The Stork Club, El Morocco and Larue.

When you are tired of all the fishing,
Climb the trail behind the hill.
There you leave the camp behind you,
Life is calm and still.

Would you change the peace and quiet
For the other hectic strife?
Does the rush and dazzle lure you
Or do you love the simple life?

Do you long for "El Morocco",
Or a conga at "The Stork"
Or does the river's murmur lull you,
As it rushes from "The Fork"?

Do you wish champagne bubbling
From a glass at "21",

Or would you sip the river, foaming
As it tears down through "The Run"?

Do you crave ice cream sodas
At Schrafts in glasses high
Or would you want to be nurtured
By Mrs. Steeves' cream pie?

When there's salmon on the table,
Or steak or cheese fondue,
Do you think you'd like it better
If you had it at "Larue"?

Do you sigh for dear, old Belmont
With the horses racing by,
Or is your love of horseflesh solaced
By "Dusty" and by "Fly"?

Taken in 1939, this photo shows Russell Murray with a fine catch. Ivan Firth stands on the right.

Fish, Flies and Fishing

*In general, by today's standards, salmon fishing at
Boland Brook Camp remained good in the
1950s, 1960s and 1970s. . .*

. . .with variations from year to year usually related to excessively high or low water, particularly if this occurred during prime time of the fishing season in July and the first ten
days of August. The ratio of salmon caught to grilse caught remained about the same, but
since those years there has been a progressive increase in the percent of the total made
up by grilse, so that now the ratio has become about one salmon to three grilse.
Interestingly enough, in 2003 the usual ratio was reversed with three salmon hooked for
every grilse, an occurrence resulting from a very large run of grilse in 2002.

Dr. George Frederick Clarke, the New Brunswick historian and archeologist, in his
book, Six Salmon Rivers and Another (Brunswick Press, Fredericton, NB, 1966), states,
"Save for a rare twenty pounder, the average Upsalquitch salmon does not go over nine
or ten pounds." Writing today, Dr. Clarke would have to revise that statement. Since the
1970s salmon in the Upsalquitch have usually weighed between seven and fourteen
pounds. Anything above fifteen pounds was considered a really big fish, worthy of some
sort of special reward, especially since anglers tend to have sensitive egos that benefit
from massaging, when it comes to their piscatorial accomplishments. All of this leads me
to the Boland Brook Camp tradition of "wall fish" and the "Wall of Fame".

From the very first year the camp was in operation (1937), any fisherman who
landed a salmon of fifteen pounds or more was entitled to a "wall fish". A paper tracing
was made of the actual trophy fish's outline and then a cutout from the tracing was labo-
riously made with a jigsaw from a thin, pine board. Aunt Allie would artistically adorn
the cut-out with eyes, mouth and fin markings, plus the salmon's weight, the angler's

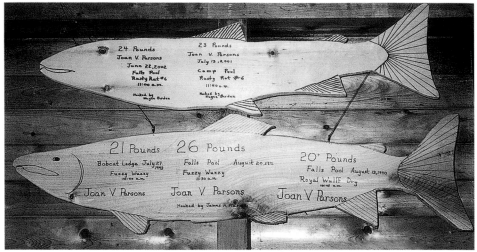

Joan Parsons' wall fish.

name, and in slightly smaller letters, the date, the pool in which it was caught and the fly that did the trick. In recent times, sometimes a salmon positively identified as a female, excuse me, a "hen", would also have eyelashes added. The finished product would then be hung on the living room wall in the main building. Since space became a premium and more large fish were caught in later years, the minimum weight for recognition was moved up to twenty pounds around 1965.

Wallace W. Turnbull and his wife, Marjory, of West Orange, New Jersey, were close friends of Allie. They fished every year at Boland Brook with uncontrolled enthusiasm. Wallace was born in Rothesay, New Brunswick, where his distinguished father, Rupert Turnbull, was the inventor of the variable pitch propeller. Wallace was a fisherman who took pleasure in every cast, and it was a fitting reward that he became involved in an epic struggle on July 4, 1950. He had hooked a twenty-five-pound salmon in The Falls pool at 8:15 a.m. and landed it at 1:15 p.m. three quarters of a mile down river. When the huge fish was finally lifted out of the water in his guide's net, Wallace was surrounded by a crowd since, when he and his guide did not return for lunch, all in camp knew that something was up and taken off down river to see what in the world was going on. The fish, a wall fish if there ever was one, remained the camp record until 1972. The salmon was foul hooked on a size 2 Black Rat, which was firmly imbedded on his snout between the eyes. More amazing still is the fact that the fly was tied to a 4 ¾-pound test gut leader. Where that leader is now, I am unaware, but I suspect it may be in the Smithsonian Institute.

My wife, Joan, has five "wall fish", including a twenty-six-pounder, caught and released on August 20, 1991 on a Fuzzy Wuzzy dry fly. Her guide was Jim Murray, then our head guide and camp manager, who died of a heart attack later that evening. Joan's fish tied the record set in 1976 by Dr. Taylor Smith of Boston. These two fish remained the camp record for many years. Dr. Fred VanPoznak (my good friend from medical school days) of London, England, has five "wall fish", including the current camp record of thirty pounds set in 1998. I have two "wall fish", but I am sure this is a practical concession, on my part, due to the decreasing availability of wall space.

During the 1950s Boland Brook anglers started to investigate fishing with "a dry", a technique more or less forgotten since the days of Monell, Hewitt and LaBranche. At that time, dry-fly fishing for The King of Game Fish was not common in the rivers of eastern Canada, nor for that matter in Iceland and Scandinavia. Our guides at Boland Brook first viewed a floating fly with a jaundiced eye, but before very long they were reluctantly trying the new technique and augmenting their fishing skills. We all appreciated that the smashing "take" of a salmon coming up from the depths to engulf a dry was the acme of satisfaction and the greatest thrill in an intriguing (and intermittently exciting) sport.

Lee Wulff's White, Grey and Royal Wulffs were initially the most productive dries, but after a while nothing ever came close to the success of the home-grown Fuzzy Wuzzy. Allie learned to tie salmon flies from the well-known and somewhat eccentric Alec Rogan, who taught at the old Alex Taylor's sporting goods store on 42nd street in New York City and then at The Angler's Roost in the same city. She became so proficient, tying wet flies during the winters in her New York apartment, that she was commissioned by Abercrombie and Fitch to provide salmon flies for sale in its angling department.

Dry flies seemed to be more difficult for her to tie and in the summer of 1950, while tying some uncooperative deer hair on a salmon hook, things self destructed with the hair splaying out of control in all directions. Considering it a weird and unusable aberration, of no interest to any self-respecting salmon, she relegated it to a distant recess in one of her many fly boxes. On one of those days when nothing, wet or dry, was able to move a fish from its lie, she tied the aberration on and threw it out on the water. You all know what happened next! The fly was christened the Fuzzy Wuzzy and to this day it continues to catch more fish than any other dry at Boland Brook.

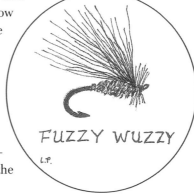

FUZZY WUZZY

L.P.

Three years ago it was my turn to concoct another major performer, tied with a white wool body, white hackles and an elongated wing of dense polar bear hair – the Polar Bear. For the first time in many years the Fuzzy Wuzzy had a competitor in the Polar Bear, which seemed to out-fish the "Fuzzy" in the evenings.

For many years, Mr. J.C. Arsenault, a renowned producer of salmon flies, had a shop in Atholville on the outskirts of Campbellton, New Brunswick, where he and his daughters supplied anglers from all over the region (see advertisement on page 55). As did most other anglers in the area, as a young man, I considered it mandatory to pay him a visit at least once every summer. On several occasions I was offered a free selection of salmon flies, if I would just let him take a quick look at a Fuzzy Wuzzy. Allie never wanted us to show the pattern to anyone, and, although I did not really support her stance on this, I followed the party line, until her death many years later, because I knew the penalties for breaking ranks could be severe.

The most frequently asked questions of anglers seem to be: "What fly were you using?" or "What did you catch him on?" Over the years at Boland Brook we have progressed from using the beautiful and traditional Scottish wet-fly patterns to the Canadian hair-fly modifications and from there to include the Green Machine and the Buck Bugs in our inventory. Likewise the Bombers have been added to our dry-fly boxes, among the Fuzzy Wuzzies and Polar Bears. On the Upsalquitch, these are probably all the dry flies you will need, particularly if the Bombers are orange or tan.

Salmon on various rivers do not seem to be attracted to the same flies. I have also been amazed to find, on some rivers, that salmon will almost never take a fly unless fished with a riffle hitch; on the Upsalquitch it is a rare salmon that will come to a hitched fly. For wet flies I think most anglers at Boland Brook would recommend the Green Highlander, the Blue Charm, Green Machine, Black Bear-Green Butt, Silver Rat and that all-time favorite performer, the Rusty Rat. Personally, I am convinced that rather than specific colors and patterns, that fly size, silhouette (configuration) and brightness/contrast are the most important in the effectiveness of various flies. There is considerable evidence that salmon do not distinguish bright colors, when the visual image of a fly has to traverse several feet of water to reach the fish; this would tend to support my belief.

This is a book about Boland Brook Camp, but this may be a good place, while I am talking about flies, fish and fishing, to mention some of my thoughts on fly fishing for Atlantic salmon, particularly as they apply to Upsalquitch River salmon. These are thoughts acquired and reinforced by many years of salmon fishing in eastern Canada, but I would hasten to add that anyone who lays down a hard-and-fast rule about the behaviour of Atlantic salmon, is probably going to find that rule broken on their next salmon fishing trip.

The angler who fishes productive waters with both wet and dry flies will double the amount of rises and "takes" encountered, when compared to fishing with wet flies only. Atlantic salmon will take dries early in the season as well as late in the season; they will take them in high water and low water. They will take them in moderately cloudy water. If you can just make out indistinct outlines of rocks on the bottom, that is clear enough. It has been in spoken word and in print that the differential temperatures of the air and the water is an important factor in success in dry fly fishing and that one must be colder or warmer than the other. I can never remember which, because it does not appear to be important. Neither is the barometric pressure, the phase of the moon, or the alignment of celestial bodies. Unfortunately, the *Farmer's Almanac* cannot be relied upon either. Tides can be important only if you are fishing in those pools that are near the river mouth. The days that the Indians' nets are in the water, or are not in the water, at the river mouth is very important.

My experience is that a dry fly must be fished on an absolute dead drift with no riffling of the fly on the surface and no pulling of the current on the fly or leader. This, I am aware, is not true on some rivers in Laborador, Newfoundland and Russia, where a riffled or skated dry fly will produce results. Even a riffled wet fly will (almost) never raise a salmon on the Upsalquitch. The only exception to this rule that I can recall, is a salmon raised by Wilf Carter, Past President and CEO of the Atlantic Salmon Federation. But

Wilf is such a friend of Atlantic salmon, that I believe the salmon know it and react accordingly. Furthermore, he is an excellent salmon fisherman.

Salmon will not take a dry fly fished below the surface of the water, as you do a wet fly. Before you explode out of your chair to contradict this statement, let me say that, occasionally, as a dry fly is being pulled off the water for a new cast, that the fly will be pulled under the surface and that a salmon will attack the fly at that moment. This is a fish that had already started up from the bottom, having started to make its move while the fly was still floating on the surface. In addition, I have never ever seen a salmon rise to a butterfly or other insect floating on the surface, to a floating leaf or to a discarded cigarette butt. There may be some of you that have, but countless times I have watched these seemingly enticing objects float (at a dead drift, mind you) over uninterested and un-reacting salmon.

A large "raise" of water, say six inches or more, will usually and temporarily have an adverse effect on successful fishing, but when the water level starts to recede, I am convinced that this is a time when fishing will probably improve. A large "raise" may also bring into the river system all those fish that we always hear are waiting in the estuary. But don't plan your fishing trip by carefully weighing all the possible positive factors against any negative factors calculated to be exerting their effects during a specific week. Just go on your trip and enjoy it – enjoy the beauty of the river you are fishing, the give and take of comfortable companionship with guides and friends, the relaxation, the escape from responsibilities. These are rewards that will soften the disappointment of poor fishing.

The best fishing advice I may have ever received came from Richard Adams, the renowned, senior guide on the Matapedia River in Quebec. I had just asked him what I might best do to catch a salmon in his river, with which I was not familiar. Without a second's hesitation he said: "Get your fly in the water". At Boland Brook Camp many salmon have been played and landed in conversation on the porch, but none have ever been hooked there. For that you have to get on the river and "get your fly in the water"!

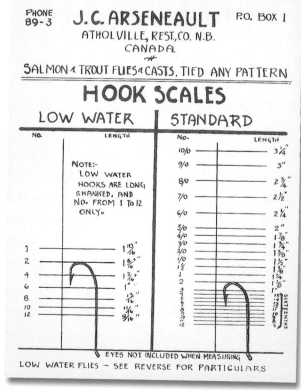

Fig. 6: Back of card advertising J.C. Arseneault's shop, circa 1940s.

The Spruce Budworm

*he Spruce Budworm may not be something that has
turned your life around or given you great
insight into who you are, but it was very important
to anyone on the Upsalquitch River in the years 1951 to 1953.*

In 1949, provincial foresters became alarmed by an increase in the number of spruce and balsam fir trees in the New Brunswick woods, specifically the Upsalquitch water-shed, that were infested by the Spruce Budworm. In 1950 some 200 square miles of these valuable trees (valuable for timber) were stripped of new foliage, and in 1951 some 2,200 square miles of trees had become infested. The large forest area in question was part of the vast Crown lands on which the International Paper Company (the "IP") had timbering rights and when Big Daddy is worried, government pays attention.

Budworm moths emerge in late June or July to lay their tiny eggs on the under-side of the needles of the evergreen trees, approximately 250 eggs per female moth. In another ten days the eggs hatch into larval stage worms. The larvae then move toward the crowns of the trees where they select a site to spend the winter in a sheltering web of silken material. When spring comes, the dormant worms emerge from their protec-tive coverings and voraciously feed on old needles and unopened buds at the tips of the branches, where the new growth is occurring. As many as 250,000 budworms could be found on a single tree and the potential existed for the worms to kill the tree over the course of several years. The spruce budworm is an intimidating adversary, as its scientific name, *Choristoneura tortricidae*, will tell you. It is the most formidable defo-liator of spruce and fir in Canada and the northern United States, and that is not a good thing to say about anything or anyone. Up to that time, no method of budworm control was known; the worm could only destroy itself when it ran out of food and when the normal checks and balances of an ecosystem took effect.

War was declared on the budworm on September 23, 1951, and the Provincial Government of New Brunswick and the New Brunswick International Paper Company became allies in a forest spraying operation of a magnitude never previously attempted. The Battle of the Budworm had been joined. Naturally Boland Brook Camp was concerned. The battle was being waged in our backyard.

The plan of attack was to spray by air some 200,000 acres of infested forest in early June when the larvae would be feeding. This left eight months to prepare the attack. An airfield of two runways on a sixty-acre location had to be bulldozed out of the bush, quarters built for foresters, aviators and entomologists, 150 people in all. A site was selected deep in the headwaters of the Upsalquitch River watershed. Sixty-five miles of woods road had to be bulldozed to join the new Budworm City with the railhead and the International Paper Company's newsprint mill at Dalhousie near Campbellton, New Brunswick. Over this road, building materials, supplies, fuel and 4,500 drums of DDT spray were hauled in sub-freezing weather.

DDT stands for Dichlorodiphenyl-trichlorethylene, a chemical that a German chemist in 1939 first recognized as a potent nerve poison for insects. The compound had been known since the previous century, but its insecticidal properties had not been known prior to 1939. The compound had been used extensively in World War II by the axis and by the allies. It had been particularly effective in the South Pacific in controlling the insect vector for malaria. The dangers of DDT were not recognized until Rachel Carson published her landmark book, Silent Spring, in 1962. She outlined the dangers occurring when DDT entered the food chain, causing reproductive dysfunction, of which the best-known example was the thin eggshells in birds.

In the spring of 1952, all the aviation fuel and DDT spray were stored in Budworm City. Pilots and their two-wing, single-engine Stearman crop dusters had arrived. Many of the pilots were combat veterans from World War II, barnstormers, racers and stunt men. On June 13, the entomologists felt the worms were at the proper stage of development and for the next fifteen days everyone worked long hours to get the task done. Chemically-treated squares of paper had been distributed over the areas to be sprayed, 22,000 in all. These squares would record the density of spray droplets in each small area. Results were plotted daily on a master chart in the control center. Before long, dying budworms were dripping down on shining silk threads everywhere. Billions of budworms were destroyed and it was estimated that more than 99.8% of the insects were killed in the sprayed areas.

The unprecedented effort was deemed so successful that plans were made to expand the spraying during the next two seasons. The New Brunswick Provincial Government and the four major timber companies with timbering rights in the province joined to form Forest Protection, Limited, a non-profit corporation. 1,000,000 acres would be sprayed in 1953 and more airfields carved out of the forest for a larger fleet of planes. The huge undertaking was felt to have been a colossal success. Was there a down side? Had success been achieved at a cost? Was Rachel Carson's warning too late?

In 1973, the use of DDT was banned by law in the United States and at some later date in Canada. DDT is a very stable compound and does not degrade in the outdoor environment. It tends to accumulate in the tissues of birds and animals, including humans, and to kill useful insects and insects that are food sources for birds. Environmental assessments before and after such projects were not required in those days. Some questions can be asked. Would the forests have survived without the spraying? What deleterious effects were inflicted on fish and birds? Were our salmon fry and parr finding fewer insects on which to feed? Might not nature have corrected this situation itself, as she so often does when an ecosystem gets out of balance? At Boland Brook camp one summer after the spraying, we noticed a gray-brown scum on the river bottom, except in those areas where the river current was the fastest. The gin-clear river (vodka-clear, if you still prefer) would also be filled with small, fibrous particles after each heavy rain. Was it real or imagined that many at camp felt there were fewer songbirds around and less blackflies and no-see-ums? The late 1950s salmon catches at Boland Brook were certainly not among our high years. Scientific investigators documented that the insects in the diet of juvenile salmon changed to accommodate to the depletion of various insects by the spraying and decreased returns of adult salmon to several rivers correlated with spraying in the previous years. The decreased returns were thought to be related to the direct toxic effects of DDT and the indirect effect of diminishing the food supply.

It is of more than casual interest that in 1999 a group of scientists from the Canadian Department of Fisheries and Oceans (W.L. Fairchild, S.B. Brown and A. Moore) clearly documented an adverse relationship between a pesticide called Matacil 1.8D, dissolved in a nonylphenol compound, which is an endocrine-disrupting chemical, that interferes with salmon survival in the sea, primarily by interfering with the ability of the fish to physiologically adapt to salt water when coming from freshwater rivers. Reduced ocean survival correlated with those river areas that had been sprayed. Matacil 1.8D is no longer used for spraying. Did salmon take it on the chin a second time? I wonder if we were not amiss in doing some objective studies at Boland Brook in 1953 to 1955. Those were the years I was overseas working for Uncle Sam, unfortunately.

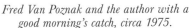

Fred Van Poznak and the author with a good morning's catch, circa 1975.

Crime

s previously described, Boland Brook Camp was isolated, without road access and without many of the utilities and deluxe comforts of most fishing camps and clubs.

Matapedia, Quebec and Campbellton, New Brunswick, were about thirty miles away and Dalhousie, New Brunswick, was a smaller community beyond Campbellton.

By way of additional preface, I need to inform you that Allie's view of bathing differed from many of her male guests. For her, the minimum requirement for cleanliness was a daily bath or shower. My father, male friends and I had the perception that isolation at a semi-rustic camp deep in the New Brunswick woods made a daily bath much less a priority than devotion to salmon fishing, eating, relaxing, or even smoking an occasional cigar.

The main lodge has only cold running water, so full bathing was limited to one bathroom in the nearby kitchen building, where there was, and still is, a cast-iron tub. The hot water came from a reservoir heated by the stove on the other side of bathroom wall. Allie did not feel swimming in the Upsalquitch River obviated the daily bathing requirement. Although she did not aggressively enforce her bathing requirement, she did infer in the presence of all, on at least one occasion, that her nephew might just be wetting his towel and leaving it in a rumpled condition on the rack to give a false impression of use. In 1975 this tense family situation prompted the following anonymous entry in the camp chronicle (a precious book in which all major camp events and artistic eruptions are entered) under the heading of "Crime."

"In the 1972 presidential election, Watergate was the issue of foremost concern in all the public opinion polls. It was but the most flagrant example of what had become increasingly apparent to all of us –– a general lessening of moral values, or more positively stated, an increase in crime. It would seem that virtue and integrity are not only un-rewarded, but have become either unrecognizable or no longer admired.

"We may think of this as an American or U.S. problem, so, perhaps, it may be unsettling to find that widespread crime does not respect international borders and that something new and sinister had become ingrained (no pun intended) in the woods of eastern Canada. Poaching, the illegal netting of salmon, had struck at the very hearts of salmon fishermen in New Brunswick and hopefully had reached its zenith, but in 1975 there appeared an even more despicable form of human behavior, a crime so heinous as to seem beyond belief.

"When the first rumors were heard, the reaction was widespread horror mixed with dis-belief. No one seemed to remember where he had heard it, as if to be unwilling to give any credence to the reports. As the last days of June turned into July, it was no longer a barely audible whisper amongst the closest of friends. It was heard by a "sport" from his guide at the railroad station in Campbellton, from a government official late one night in a Dalhousie bar, as he conversed with his friends, and from a Matapedia River "guardien" working hard to consume an excess of Molson's ale in the back room of the Hotel Matapedia. It was even heard in the hallowed halls of that piscatorial sanctum sanctorum, the Restigouche Salmon Club: "You know they have always been the most respected fishing camp in these parts. No one there is ever allowed to catch more than his legal limit, fish without a license, use an ille-gal lure. Why they even enter every fish in a book and grilse are always returned to the river. They have never fished on Sundays!" But then the damning words were spoken: "You may not believe it, but they are wetting the towels at Boland Brook!!"

"Now before a wave of horror and revulsion overwhelms the saddened reader, let him consider some points that might be raised in mitigation. Washing, or if you prefer, bathing has always been anathema to the veteran angler or woodsman. He regards bathing much as a cobra regards the mongoose, the soldier a landmine, Count Dracula a shining cross. It may well be related to the fact that in the woods, water is often a scarce commodity and too valuable to waste on the human integument, or a commodity too lacking in importance, when the pools are full and the salmon "taking." Medicine, too, has warned of the danger of too vigorously attacking our primary defense against bacterial invasion with the excess use of soap and water. A good layer of insect repellent, caked dust, desquamated epithelial cells and miscellaneous, adherent debris from swamp, pine needles and campfire smoke has an undeniable protective, medicinal value.

"The rules at Boland Brook are strict, surveillance keen, but it was being done. Three, or even four, may have been suspected, but whomever the criminal elements were, they stuck together, each loath to identify the other. Towels were being wetted down and rum-pled and even a washcloth here and there, although no bath was drawn nor body scrubbed. It may have been done in the dark of night, a furtive figure sneaking into the bathroom, a muffled unlatching of the door, work being done in utter darkness, risking the chance for a return invitation to Boland Brook. The entire ghastly story has yet to unfold.

"To what depths can human behavior sink? What does the future hold? It may be that at some future date historians will write of Boland Brook Camp, that it was there that they first wet the towels."

CHAPTER

14

Crisis

*I first visited "Aunt Allie" at Boland Brook Camp
with my father, Livingston Parsons, in 1937 and
from that point forward Boland Brook Camp
and Atlantic salmon became two of the most
important and rewarding parts of my life.*

Even though I felt Allie always viewed me as a boy still wet behind the ears and as one whose opinions were only of value if they were in regard to medicine, over the years I became more and more aware of the strong bond that had developed between us — something more than a family tie or just affection.

A major event occurred at Boland Brook camp in 1982. This was at a time when I was increasingly busy with an active surgical practice in Albuquerque, and when my wife, Joan, and I were raising our three active children, Livy III, David and Denise. Actually, Joan was doing the lion's share of the raising. In the 1980s, the three children were in college or establishing careers—the boys in the financial arena in New York City and Denise in the clothing industry in Dallas. You have previously read about my wife's fishing ability, but Allie, who really did not have too much use for small children, allowed our three to first come to Boland Brook between age eleven to thirteen and all three have become ardent and accomplished salmon fishermen. Every year all of us spent vacation time at Boland Brook and we still do.

Allie often referred to the Parsons Jr. family as "a mob", perhaps in some way suggesting a comparison to Alec Guiness' infamous "Lavender Hill Mob" from the 1951 film, though we carried no violin cases, just a smattering of rod cases and a few shapeless duffel bags. For me, each year I have looked at my week or ten days at Boland

Brook as a complete change of scene and escape from the demands and pressures of surgery. Flying to New Brunswick from Albuquerque was never possible, so relaxation started on the overnight train, the Ocean Limited, from Montreal to Matapedia, Quebec, where the head guide, Russell Murray and later his son, Jim, would meet us in the pre-dawn light around 4:45 a.m. In the camp truck we would cross the bridge spanning the lower Restigouche River, motor up along the New Brunswick side of the river before turning inland to the Upsalquitch, where we would be taken up river the final five miles by canoe to camp. After settling in the canoe, I would light my pipe, breathe in the air filled with the aromas of river and woods and enjoy the river sounds and the wildlife seen along the way. There was an additional bonus crossing from Quebec into New Brunswick, because the time changed from eastern daylight savings time to Atlantic daylight savings time, an hour later, which had an immediate invigorating effect to know it was six o'clock and not five o'clock.

It was not a remotely usual year, 1981. In late June I was in the operating room in Albuquerque removing a highly malignant tumor, a leiomyosarcoma of the small intestine. Sarcomas are uncommon malignancies that arise from bone, muscle or soft tissues; in this case the "leiomyo" referred to the muscular layer of the intestinal wall. The circulating nurse came up to tell me that I had an urgent call from Cambellton, New Brunswick. Apprehensive as I was, I did not feel I could divert attention from my patient, under anesthesia and in mid-operation, so asked that I be allowed to return the

Livy Parsons, Katharine Parsons, and Jim Murray on the Upsalquitch River, 1984.

call as soon as possible. When the abdominal closure was well underway, I left completion of the operation to my assistant surgeon and returned the call. Allie, who was eighty-three years old, was in Soldiers Memorial Hospital in Campbellton as a result of a heart attack, her survival far from being assured. "Dr. Fred" VanPoznak, my dear friend since medical school days, had been in camp and had taken her to the hospital. She had been casting at The Falls, when she slumped to the bottom of her small, sixteen-foot canoe, falling half way over the side as she fell. Jim Murray, who could not swim a stroke, was able to grasp her before the canoe tipped over and poled the canoe back to camp. This canoe was too small to accommodate an outboard motor. Unconscious, she was put in a sleeping bag and taken down river by canoe to "the landing" at the end of the Upsalquitch River road, where an ambulance was waiting to transport her to the hospital.

Livy Parsons on the Boland Brook ATV, 1982. The home-made trailer was not hitched up the night of the harrowing trail trip to Upsalquitch Village.

I told "Dr. Fred" and Dr. Wardekar, the cardiologist at the hospital, that I was on my way.

It took me almost thirty-six frantic hours to reach the hospital, where Dr. Wardekar met me outside the four-bed intensive care unit to tell me my aunt was moving a little and might be able to hear what was being said, but that she was semi-comatose and essentially unresponsive. I should not expect her to recognize my presence. Moving quickly to the bedside, I took her hand and said, Allie, it's Livy; I am here." She opened her eyes and said, "Damit, Livy, it took you long enough to get here." I had never heard her swear before, nor have I since. It is still hard for me to recall this scene without emotion. Dr. Wardekar said these were the first words she had spoken.

To say the very least, things were unsettled at Boland Brook, so later that afternoon Jim took me up river to talk to the very concerned staff, Peggy Murray (Jim's wife), Jean Ryan (our cook), Bud Polack (our other guide), Chris MacDougal (our chore boy) and "Dr. Fred". It was a very subdued fishing camp. That evening it began to pour rain in sheets, as only it can in New Brunswick. At 10:00 p.m. our radio-telephone rang with Dr. Wardekar on the line. Allie's pulse had fallen to a rate of thirty-five, dangerously low. Once again I was on the way to the hospital, but it was a black, rainy night, much too dangerous to negotiate rapids and submerged rocks by going down river by canoe. All in camp were awake the instant the phone rang, I yelled to Bud Pollack to gas up our ATV (all terrain vehicle) and for he and "Dr. Fred" to put on their rain suits. There was a marginal trail that started behind the camp and wound eight miles through the woods, over bogs, mud holes and steep hills with washouts, to eventually reach the end of the Upsalquitch River Road. While "Dr. Fred" and Bud hung on for dear life, I drove that four-wheeler as fast as I dared and faster than anyone should have, with the rain beating down on us, mud splashing and skidding wildly. Three people will never forget that ride; two passengers were scared to death. We reached Upsalquitch Village, ran from the four-wheeler to the truck for the twenty-eight-mile drive to Campbellton, arriving at the hospital at midnight. The three doctors agreed a pacemaker was what was needed and Dr. Wardekar said one, and only one, was available in the hospital stock room. Dr. Wardekar said, "I have never put in a pacemaker." I responded, "Neither have I, but I have seen it done and we are going to do it tonight. Let's get her to the operating room right now." It never occurred to me that I did not have a license to practice in Canada and, fortunately, no one has ever brought the matter up.

But we got the job done that night and Allie stabilized and made steady improvement for about five days, at which time she developed signs of intestinal obstruction. The local surgeon felt surgical exploration was mandatory, but I felt her obstruction was due to a prolonged period of low blood pressure immediately after her initial attack and that her gastrointestinal tract was responding to the injury incurred when her gut was receiving an inadequate perfusion of blood. We both sweated this out, neither conceding to the other's point of view. After four days of unbelievable tension, Allie's situation improved and moved on to complete resolution. Four years of medical school and four years of surgical post-graduate training would have been worth it, even if she were the only patient I ever treated.

Three weeks later Allie was moved back to Boland Brook Camp, where my wife, Joan, an extremely capable R.N., had arrived to help her convalesce. Joan was assistant head nurse the year she graduated from nursing school on the Surgical Service at Roosevelt Hospital in New York City, where I was a surgical resident. No sooner had things settled down with Allie back at her beloved camp than a major forest fire started moving north across New Brunswick. Although it was fifty miles away, the Department of Natural Resources demanded that all camps on the Upsalquitch be evacuated. I could not convince the authorities that we owned the camp and the land that it was on, that we were not leasing from the Provincial Government and that we should be treated as other homeowners were being treated in nearby Upsalquitch and Robinsonville, where evacuation was not being mandated. Besides, I urged to no avail that we had a recovering heart patient, who could ill afford to be moved around. In desperation I called the then Minister of the Department of Natural Resources, Bud Bird, a man whom I knew only from his reputation and accomplishments. It was really a surprise when our radio mobilphone rang several hours later with Bud Bird on the line, saying he understood our situation and would take care of it. We were allowed to stay, but for some reason no one could understand, no one could fish on the river. In about another ten days to two weeks the fire was out, and although those at camp could smell the smoke, there was no danger. It is interesting that in recent years Bud Bird and I have gotten to be the best of friends.

By this time I had returned to Albuquerque having endured endless flak from my parents and sisters, who insisted I charter a plane to return my aunt to her home in New York City. Allie insisted she had no intention of leaving Boland Brook, that she was getting the best of care, and if an emergency came up, it would take just as long to get her to the hospital in Campbellton as it would to get across town in rush hour from her apartment in New York City to Roosevelt Hospital. Frankly, I agreed with her. Besides, who wants to try to move the Rock of Gibraltar.

Allie's recovery continued and Joan took her home to New York at the end of the summer. All of that summer remains etched in my memory. I also will always remember Allie telling me as she left the hospital: "That was a very bad time for me to have done what I did (meaning having a heart attack), I was fishing at The Falls and just had a good rise."

Joan Parsons playing a salmon at The Falls in 1999, with Wayne Borden as her guide.

CHAPTER

15

Fauna

Close contact with nature has been a bonus to the pleasure of fishing for Atlantic salmon.

Something should be said about the wildlife that lives above the surface of the water, the animals and birds with which we have shared the woods for sixty-five summers, the true owners of the area on whose land we trespass without formal permission.

Moose, the largest and most impressive of the local residents, have been seen in increasing numbers over the last twenty years, displacing deer sightings in frequency, perhaps, as a result of the forest's recovery from the devastation of the forest fires in the 1920s and 1930s. These large ungulates are now seen frequently each summer, most commonly wading in the river above and below the camp and in the beaver pond up the hill a half-mile behind the camp. Recently two bulls and a cow and her calf were often seen peacefully munching water plants in the beaver pond. It is not unusual for a moose to wander among the camp buildings or to check out the garden. In fact, two years ago a young calf, lost or abandoned by its mother, stayed around the immediate environs of the camp for the better part of a week, becoming almost tame, since we could approach to within ten yards of him (her?). He seemed to enjoy watching us as much as we enjoyed watching him. One day, as quickly as he had arrived, the moose calf left. We wondered if one of the moose who visit the camp now in the summer is our old friend.

Bears always seem to get the most attention. Every camp has its bear stories and Boland Brook Camp has been no exception. They are seen along the river, sometimes swimming across it, on the trail up to the beaver pond and, on more occasions than I would like to mention, right in the camp. Before it was declared against the law, we used to burn our disposable trash and bury what could not be burned, which may have

Cow moose parading through Boland Brook Camp, 1999.

been of interest to the bears. In the 1970s a bear looked in the windows of the guide house, something many guests were interested in doing, but lacking in the necessary nerve. The Shadow was too old to have been suspected and the bear's visit was established through more than the usual hearsay, by muddy paw and claw prints on the windowsill.

The most remarkable bear visitation came early one morning in 1971 when the camp was awakened by a commotion in the kitchen, a commotion that included screams from the cook, who was on her way to start the morning breakfast. The first investigators on the scene found little left of the back screen door, the entire kitchen in disarray and a self-satisfied bear in residence. The uninvited guest bolted through the front screen door, which resulted in two screen doors needing to be repaired and a new policy to close all the wood doors to the kitchen at night, as well as the screen doors.

Last summer we arrived at camp in June to find a dead cow moose on the river-bank near The Falls. Almost every evening, as we fished The Falls a large bear would arrive to feed on the carcass. The spectacle was diverting, but after a few days the smell became an olfactory disaster. That same summer we saw a cub several times around the camp, usually as we were going through the trees to or from the river. This did make us a little nervous, since we felt sure mama must be nearby watching.

No one was ever threatened by a bear, but I am sorry to say that once it was neces-sary to shoot a large black bear. Allie was sometimes, by her definition, left alone in camp, meaning no men were about, since the guides and their "sports" were on the river fishing. On several successive evenings, a bear ambled by the porch of the main building where she was sitting, unnerving her greatly. All agreed, with one dissenting vote (mine), that the bear should be shot. I was not overly upset, since I am a Republican in New Mexico and used to being in the minority and being out-voted.

In the early years at camp in August we would often be poled up river in the afternoons to Rock Pool, which was just above the Boland Brook Camp water, to pick blueberries from the sunny, south-facing hillside, which was then devoid of any trees. Bears enjoyed this same activity and it was not unusual to have to scare off two or three before we disembarked from our canoes. You will recall that I had acquired a bear license previously on a week-long trip up river, when, surprisingly, and in retrospect fortunately, no bears were seen.

Guide Jim Murray and the author's oldest son Livy Parsons III with the ill-fated bear, 1972.

Birds seem to be everywhere on the river and in the surrounding woods, some well known to us at home, such as robins, ravens, hawks, flickers and barn swallows, but others we see only at "camp". These birds include flycatchers, beautiful black and yellow grosbeaks and several species of humming-birds and woodpeckers, including the rare pileated woodpecker. Along the river there are kingfishers, plovers, mergansers, black duck and an occasional eider duck. Frequently a lone seagull or two will fly up the river from the Bay of Chaleur looking for dead fish to eat. We do not oblige them. We have also been excited to see bald eagles and once a golden eagle in the past five years. These magnificent birds soar high in the sky above us or sit in a tall pine tree not too far from where we are fishing. Another bird we hear, but do not see, is the Peabody Bird whose somewhat mournful "Peabody-Peabody-Peabody" cry provokes thoughtfulness and reverie. I am not sure, but this bird may be the white-throated sparrow. As you can tell I am not your basic "birder", but we have had at least two in camp and they have identified and recorded over forty different bird species.

To return to mammals, foxes, mink, otters skunks, raccoons, rabbits and ground-hogs give us cause for excitement. Chipmunks are everybody's favorite and one year we had a family nest in our woodshed. By July you could sit quietly on the logs and they would eat out of your hand, scurrying around your shoulders. A few times we have had to deal with exotics, such as a seal on two occasions and once with a bobcat seen on a rock ledge just below the Frying Pan pool. This ledge extends out at a right angle to the river, where a small brook enters just as the river sweeps at a sharp angle to the left forming a short, deep pool before the granite ledge tapers off and the water shallows out. It is a favorite spot for salmon to lie, while grilse will hold in the shallow pocket above the ledge, where the brook enters. The bobcat sighting is how the pool, Bobcat Ledge, got its name.

Probably the most discussion of an "exotic" concerned the sightings of a mountain lion, or panther. At the considerable risk of being tagged as sexist, it seemed to me that these reports were uniformly being filed by women, who, at the end of an evening's fishing were walking up the short, dark trail through the woods which allowed the guides to pole their canoe up around the rapids at the head of Josie's pool without the extra weight of the fishermen. (This statement could cause me problems, too). One evening, after there had been a sighting on several consecutive nights, I walked the area just before dark with a flashlight and surprised a large, tawny house-cat that must have forsaken domesticity for the summer. I will not flat-out state that there are no mountain lions in the Upsalquitch Valley, but I do have a strong opinion in this regard.

Last, but not least, a word about our friends the beavers. We have always comfortably shared the river and the woods with these toothsome animals, enjoyed watching them frolic in the water, working to build their houses along the river banks, seeing them swim through our pools while we are fishing and sometimes seeing them shut off our water supply to the camp with their dams. They kept putting a dam above our water intake at the beaver pond, shutting off our water, to coin a phrase. Something drastic had to be done and Jim Murray found a good solution. A ways up Boland Brook there was a consistently wet place on a steep hillside, where he dug out a huge hole and placed a very large, wooden barrel in the ground. Water seeped into this steadily and after moving our pipe from the beaver pond to the barrel, or puncheon, as it was called, this arrangement provided a dependable supply of water thereafter. The beaver had been outwitted.

We usually have a dog at camp and there was one whose name and species escape me for the moment, that used to love to play tag with a beaver in the Camp Pool. The dog, barking furiously, would swim after the beaver, who would wait until the dog was about four feet away before slapping his tail on the water, diving and reappearing about fifty yards behind the frustrated dog, who would then swim after the beaver once again. This game would continue until the dog would drag himself up on the beach with his tongue hanging out, completely exhausted. The beaver would continue to happily cruise the river.

Not a day went by that somehow did not involve interaction with the wild fauna.

C H A P T E R

Problems

*W*ildlife *around the camp and river never caused any really serious,
deleterious or damaging situations with which we had to deal,
but the same could not be said about that most unpredictable
of mammals,* Homo sapiens *(subspecies:* bureauocraticus*).*

The first problem surfaced almost from day one, actually in February 1938 to be exact. It was rumored and then confirmed that an application was to be made to the Legislature of the Province of New Brunswick to provide for incorporation of a company to be called the Upsalquitch Water and Power Company, whose business would be development of waterpower by damming the Upsalquitch River. I do not know what it is, unless, perhaps, it is dollars, that makes humans want to dam every free-flowing, wild river, be it in the sub-arctic, New England, the Pacific Northwest, the Andes Mountains, Indonesia or God knows where. I am also ashamed to inform the reader that of the five misguided individuals who conceived this scheme for the Upsalquitch, three were health-care providers, one a physician and surgeon, one a dentist and one a druggist. The other two were an accountant and an electrical engineer. All were residents of Campbellton, New Brunswick.

Of the two sites considered for a ninety-foot dam, one was The Falls area right in the middle of the Boland Brook property, because it was there that there was the greatest drop in the river height in the smallest length of the river. In addition, there were cliffs of solid granite on each side of The Falls. No environmental survey was required for such a project in those days, and the worst scenario was that Boland Brook Camp would be deep under water with motorboats roaring over its submerged buildings. Other camps and local groups were equally concerned and lawyers were hired to represent their interests. The International Paper Company, with whom we would be dealing on other matters in the future, had only one concern, that provisions would be made to float their logs around the dam. Surveying by air and on foot, estimations of water flow and potential power that could be derived, wrangling over who had the right to do what to whom continued over several years, before the sponsors of the bill to incorporate the power company withdrew the introduction of the bill to the provincial legislature in 1950. It was thought by many that failure to raise the necessary capital was the major reason for the bill's withdrawal.

A recurrent threat to Boland Brook Camp has been mining exploration, since New Brunswick law allows prospecting on all provincial land, the only exceptions being provincial parks and Indian reservations. This meant that anyone with a prospecting license could stake out claims, work them and build the necessary access roads. There were some regulations about having to restore damage to surface of the land and not mining where there were existing buildings. The first threat came in 1972 from Noranda Mines, Ltd., Canada's largest mining company. After consultation with the District Geologist and a New Brunswick lawyer, Aunt Katharine decided to fight fire with fire. She applied for and received her own prospector's license and promptly proceeded to stake out claims on every square foot of her own Boland Brook property, a remarkably clever and effective counterattack. The Noranda CEO also received a scathing letter from one of its stockholders, completing the two-pronged attack. The Boland Brook claims had to be renewed after one year and by the end of the second year the threat had passed, so that self-staking of claims was discontinued. Nothing significant in the way of metals had been found in neighboring areas and, if Boland Brook's claims were to be renewed, it was necessary to provide some significant evidence of the claims being worked.

In 1998, a second assault on the Boland Brook property appeared. It was now my responsibility to deal with it. Wayne Borden, my head guide and camp manager, phoned me in Albuquerque to tell me that teams of two men were infiltrating our woods, tying plastic ribbons to our trees and driving stakes into the ground, Amazingly, even with maps, these men had no idea they were on private property and were just doing their job, as instructed by an exploration firm in Bathurst, New Brunswick. They were also preparing to take core samples below the ground surface, seeking gold, silver, copper, tin or iron. I called Bathurst and found out that the Bathurst exploration firm had been hired by guess who? Noranda Mines, Ltd.! A highly respected lawyer in Frederickton, New Brunswick, was contacted to protect our interests, a lawyer who agreed to work on our behalf, until I discovered another of his clients was Noranda Mines. Another well-respected lawyer and chronic Atlantic salmon fisherman (incidentally, I believe all respected Frederickton lawyers are salmon fishermen) was engaged and he informed

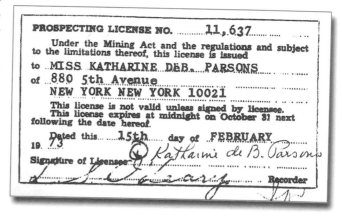

me that registered mining claims expire within two years, if the claims are not worked, and that the prospectors were within their rights in what they were doing on Boland Brook property. This time all we could do was register a strong complaint that common courtesy would have mandated notification to a landowner that his property was being invaded, that all surface damage to land and trees would have to be restored to their original condition, that all trash brought in would have to be taken out and that, furthermore, David would be monitoring every move Goliath was taking. The major concern on our part was that trees would be destroyed, roads built to bring in heavy equipment and that Boland Brook stream would be polluted with devastating effect on our dwindling salmon stocks. An extensive mining operation had been started on the headwaters of the Southeast Branch of the Upsalquitch in 1988, but it had been discontinued after a brief existence, leaving constructed forest roads and surface damage to the detriment of the region. To everyone's relief, the core samples from the Boland Brook property failed to show high enough concentrations of the sought-after metals and by the end of the summer our woods had been restored almost completely to their pre-invasion beauty.

Now, continuing on the theme of dealing with bureaucracy, it is necessary to return to our friends, the beavers. Generally speaking, Boland Brook lives in harmony with these buck-toothed workaholics, but one year the situation got completely out of hand. The beaver were cutting down the large trees stabilizing the riverbank near the camp. Allie contacted the local office of the Department of Natural Resources, that wrote a response, part of which follows:

"I would suggest that if you wrap the trunk of these trees with tar paper or with burlap bags, you might find it a success in preventing beavers from eating down any more of your trees. It might also be advised to use some deodorant such as creolin which could be put on this tar paper and burlap bags, which could drive the beavers away".

The only good thing I can say about this letter, which has been preserved for posterity, is that I greatly admire the courage of the person who signed it. Allie fired off a reply, indicating her admiration for Natural Resources' belief that an elderly lady would be physically and financially capable of wrapping thousands of trees in the New Brunswick woods and her shock in realizing this was the only solution offered. Within the week after receiving Allie's letter, Natural Resources sent up two trappers to remove the offending animals. I have always admired and learned from my Aunt's direct approach to letter writing and her skillful use of sarcasm, when she felt she had been dealt with unfairly.

Yes, we have had our problems over the years and new threats of some kind will undoubtedly arise in the future.

A trapped beaver is released at a new location, 1942.

C H A P T E R

17

Today

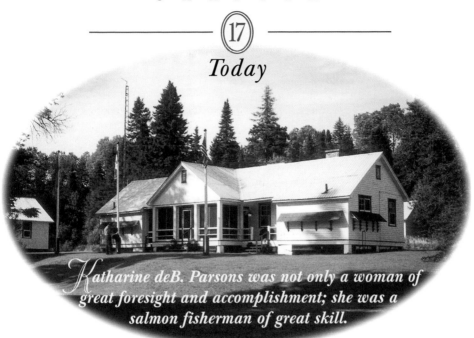

Katharine deB. Parsons was not only a woman of great foresight and accomplishment; she was a salmon fisherman of great skill.

Before you raise a politically correct eyebrow at my use of the word "fisherman" here and previously in this book, I need to tell you, if there is one thing my aunt was not, it was a woman's libber. In fact, sometime in her last year she told me: "Do not put on my tombstone *She was a good fisherwoman,* but you can say, *She was a good fisherman.*" I can assure she would have no use either for the now commonly used, gender-neutral word "fisher."

Allie was thirty-nine years old when she bought the square mile of land in Eldon Parish of Restigouche County in New Brunswick, Canada. Along with woods, beaver ponds, bogs and Boland Brook came the riparian rights on a mile and a quarter of one of eastern Canada's best and most beautiful salmon rivers, the Upsalquitch. Riparian rights mean that the owner has the sole right to decide who can fish on that segment of the river, and of course, who cannot. The river itself is a public highway and no one can be stopped from paddling or motoring through or along it. I suppose the same could be said for swimming through it.

One summer, five campers, drunk and rowdy, pulled up their canoes at the mouth of Boland Brook, where they proceeded to throw beer cans and other trash on the ground and hauled out their fishing equipment. My aunt, with head guide Jim Murray standing at her side, politely asked them to leave, stating that she owned the property and that fishing and camping were forbidden. She was immediately exposed to repeated, foul invective and asked to produce written proof of ownership. I was in camp at the time and wanted Jim to get his shotgun to make our position very clear.

Fortunately, I was again outvoted, cooler heads prevailed and a phone call was made to the Royal Mounted Police, who said they would get there as soon as they could. Because of our isolation and lack of access by road, this meant an estimated four to five hours. Boyd Noye, respected and well known to us, a warden of the Department of Natural Resources, was in the area and came to rescue us from an ugly situation. Though he had no authority to arrest or fine, he was able to quickly persuade the drunken men to leave, defusing an ugly and somewhat frightening situation.

Allie could cast well and accurately, and could hook and play a salmon with great skill. She was not a distance caster, firmly believing in the old school that says you should be able to hold a book against your body with your casting arm, using only fore-arm and wrist. She had no interest in learning the single- and double-haul maneuvers, just as she believed no shoulder motion was necessary in fly-casting. As a boy, there was no question that she taught me a lot, but as I grew older and expanded my fly-casting skills, when in her presence, I had to keep it under my Stetson. Fortunately, when we fished together in a canoe, she placed me behind her for my own safety and this also meant she could not see what I was doing. In checking over the camp record during Allie's last summer, I found she had hooked and landed over 800 salmon and grilse in her lifetime—perhaps, something for the Guinness Book of Records. She start-ed late at thirty-nine years of age, when she bought the square mile of land in Eldon Parish in Restigouche County in the Province of New Brunswick.

For many years Boland Brook Camp has remained one of only two privately-owned fishing properties on the Upsalquitch, which is fishable from its mouth, where it joins the Restigouche River, for twenty-two miles up to The Forks and up each of the two branches for ten or more miles. There are, at present, three other fishing camps on the river, which lease their water from the provincial government through a system

Guide Denis Arsenault demonstrates good catch-and-release technique, 1999.

whereby leases are granted for ten years on the basis of successful bidding at an auction held in Frederickton, New Brunswick. The last auction was in January, 2003, and none of the three previous lease owners failed to renew their leases, which I feel is a good thing for the river and its salmon population, since the lessees are all committed salmon conservationists, well attuned to the problems faced by declining runs of this extraordinary fish.

The lessees can build lodges, which they own, but they do not own the land on which the buildings are built, and when leases change hands, sale of the buildings to new lessees must be negotiated. Every tenth year when the leases come up for renewal there is the recurring threat that the leases will be discontinued and the formerly leased stretches will be put into more public water. Since 1937, twenty-nine miles have already been withdrawn from auction and are now public, or "Crown" water for the use of New Brunswick residents, who are allotted two fishing days in a first-come, first-served sign-up system that opens in March of each year. I believe removal of the remaining river leases would result in a considerable loss of income to the province, heavier fishing pressure on the fish and more water with insufficient surveillance to prevent illegal activity.

The fishing at Boland Brook Camp has not changed a lot, over the years except in the total number of fish caught. Salmon runs have been declining in the Upsalquitch River at an alarming rate, in line with what has been happening in most rivers in eastern Canada. Now a good day is when one fish is caught, and when two or more are caught, a very good day. The ratio of salmon to grilse is now almost one to three. The Camp Pool holds fish, but in nowhere near the numbers that it used to. Boland Brook has re-channeled its outlet into the main river to a point about thirty yards below where it used to enter, so that the cooler brook water hugs closer to the shore, rather than flowing out into the pool, a possible negative factor. In August, when the river temperature approaches 70 degrees F., scores of salmon will lie in the cooler brook water, where it is next to impossible to attract them to any wet or dry fly, rather than in the main current of the pool against the far bank. In Augusts now the river seems consistently warmer and lower than it used to. Excessive streamside timbering upriver and more rapid water run-off after rains are, no doubt, a factor.

The Falls pool seems to hold good numbers of fish and in the last fifteen years consistently has provided our best fishing. Below the Falls rapids, Ivan's Run has filled in with gravel and so has the upper half of Josie's Pool. Our other pools see fewer fish, but anticipation remains high, though expectancy is less. I think we fish harder, longer and, perhaps, even more skillfully, since we know the water well, to achieve the same or lesser results than in former years. On the positive side, in the last four years we are seeing more really large salmon, in the twenty- to thirty-pound range. The chance to get that "Wall Fish" is always there. Salmon-fishing tackle has improved, reels are lighter and more efficient; with the advent of graphite rods, rods have become shorter, lighter and better casting. However, I still get a special feel from cane and my nine-foot, three-inch Garrison rod is still the best dry-fly rod I have ever had the privilege of possessing. The Upsalquitch River has become better known to anglers in general and it is being fished by far more people than formerly. It is interesting that several recent books on salmon fishing have devoted many words, or even chapters, to the Upsalquitch, but none have solicited information from those of us at Boland Brook, who have fished there far the longest. Economic surveys have been done on the Restigouche River and its tributaries, and again, we are not usually even on the "complete" list of those from whom information is solicited. It is kind of nice to be a small, unknown family camp. Or is this just sour grapes?

In sixty-five years at Boland Brook things have not changed a great deal, which is probably a strong point. The camp is still isolated, an isolation that we have vigorously protected, and the camp is still unapproachable by road, requiring that the last five miles of any journey to B.B.C. be by canoe up river from the end of the river road in the village of Upsalquitch. The air is still clean, fresh and aromatic, wildlife is even more abundant than in the past, Boland Brook still runs fast and cold and the river still runs crystal clear over its bed of multi-colored rocks and gravel. Hills forested by spruce, cedar, pine and maple nestle the river in a beautiful valley unspoiled by human development.

An angled salmon being tagged with tagging gun just forward of the dorsal fin in 1993.

The camp still has no electricity, other than a small gas generator to run the washing machine and boost the charge on the battery for the telephone. There is still no heating other than the wood-burning fireplaces. There is still hot water in only one location and, thank goodness, there is no TV. The telephone has changed, not necessarily progressed, from a crank-operated, party-line phone to a radiotelephone to a cell phone, operated by a twelve-volt battery and a solar panel. The current phone is a mixed blessing because it works very well, but like so many American enterprises, it is subject to over exploitation.

The camp schedule is still unchanged: up at 7:00 a.m., when the guides, being as noisy as they can, slam an enamel jug of hot water down outside each bedroom door for washing and shaving. Fishing is still from 8:30 a.m. to noon and 6:30 p.m. to dark.

Reveille is still postponed a half-hour on Sundays to 7:30 a.m., but we do fish seven days a week. Lunch at 1:15 p.m. is still our big meal of the day, leaving us a bit wiped out until a light meal before the evening's outing. One of the few things I have had the temerity to change is the time on which the camp runs. We now run on local time, Atlantic Daylight Savings Time, rather than on Eastern Daylight Savings Time. Allie believed the world ran on New York time, but using local time makes it easier to

Canoe approaches the stretch of rapids known as The Falls, 1994.

remember train and plane arrival and departure times for our guests. Also, on his trip to town for our supplies for the coming week, our Head Guide and Camp Manager, Wayne Borden, no longer arrives in Campbellton at noon, a time when many businesses are shut in the summer for an hour or more at mid-day. The cow, the chickens, and, unfortunately, some of the salmon are gone, so our provision-gathering arrangements have been altered.

The original Boland Brook Camp buildings are all intact. The inner lining of the ice-house has been redone; the chimneys have been repaired and resealed; the kitchen-dining room building has been shored up and re-leveled; some floor areas, most outside steps and porches have been replaced; maintenance painting is required almost annually. Most of this work is done by the camp staff with some assistance by the fishermen. The camp's continued isolation still mandates a certain degree of self-sufficiency.

People and salmon have adapted to the noise of outboard motors, although our guides still carry poles and paddles in their canoes that we use for fishing and travel on the river. They retain their skills in the latter two methods of propulsion. The camp has survived an abortive plan to build a dam on the property and two invasions by prospectors looking for precious metals. We have readily adopted catch-and-release, which was started in 1984, and are even disturbed that current licenses allow for retention of too many grilse. Change and controversy continue and our salmon are caught in the middle.

Boland Brook conceived a project to study the effect of catch-and-release on salmon, to be carried out on the Upsalquitch in the mid 1990s, under the auspices of the Department of Fisheries and Oceans (DFO) and the Atlantic Salmon Federation. Many people earnestly believed that all salmon caught by fishermen and released would not survive, something subsequently proven not to be the case. Anglers and their guides were taught, prior to release, to implant numbered tags below the dorsal fin of salmon that they had played in their usual manner and brought to the net. The Upsalquitch River has a barrier pool ten miles up the northwest branch where salmon and grilse working up river to spawn could be kept and examined to see if they had been tagged and if they were in good condition. My job at Boland Brook, in addition to tagging, was to place a small radio, the size and shape of a fig, in the stomach of grilse and salmon that had been hooked and played. Each radio gave out a discrete signal, so that an investigator with a radio-receiver in his canoe could search the river on the following days, determining fish survival and location. I had a homemade gadget, not unlike a small gastroscope, through which the radios could be inserted. The study, which was largely carried out by Dr. Bruce Tufts of Queens University in Ontario and Richard Booth, a graduate student, showed that approximately ninety-five percent of the fish survived, providing that river water temperatures were below 72 degrees F. Much other useful information was also accumulated and the study subsequently reinforced by studies on other rivers. Initially there was some doubt that fishermen and

K. Parsons in 1989 at age 92 landing a salmon at Boland Brook with the help of guide Jim Murray.

guides would be able to handle the necessary techniques for tagging. Not only were they eager to participate, but pleased to be involved. The study was a landmark study in salmon conservation.

Camp Pool at Boland Brook Camp, 2002.

In the 1990s Boland Brook was also involved in satellite rearing, a conservation concept promoted by the Atlantic Salmon Federation. In the fall, several spawners were taken from the Upsalquitch River and, at the regional Charlo Fish Hatchery, eggs were taken from the female salmon and fertilized with milt from the males. During the winter and spring the eggs were hatched and the baby salmon reared until the fry stage, when they were two to two and a half inches long. At this time, around the first week in July, they were transferred to a large tank at Boland Brook Camp, which had a continuous flow of brook water through an intake pipe and an outlet drainpipe, imprinting them with Boland Brook water. The fry were fed daily over the summer and fall and we watched them grow to the parr stage, when they have brightly colored spots and vertical bands and are three to four inches in length. They were released into the Upsalquitch River in late October, when most of the fish-eating birds had left and the river water was cold enough that the trout were not actively feeding. These parr would continue their growth over several years in the river to the smolt stage, six to eight inches long, at which time they would migrate down river to the ocean and hopefully return in future years as adult grilse and salmon. The key to this program of augmenting naturally-reared wild salmon returns to the river, was using our own river-specific genetic stock, which promoted an increased chance of survival. The method is now being used by many camps around New Brunswick and appears to be moderately successful. Our fish were marked by clipping their adipose fin. Several marked grilse were caught after four years of the program, this being the usual time needed for completion of their life cycle from birth to return as adults.

End of an Era

s the years went by, Allie entered her nineties, but she continued to live for her summers at Boland Brook Camp, planning for them all through the winter and spring.

It became increasingly difficult for my wife, Joan, and I to get her from her New York apartment to the river and back. Driving from New York always took three days, driving on her schedule, with overnight stops in Augusta, Maine, and Lincoln, Maine. Another route was flying by way of Montreal to the small airport at Charlo, New Brunswick, driving forty-five miles in a truck to the river and then moving the last five miles up river by canoe. This could be accomplished in one day, but the return trip required an overnight stay in a Montreal hotel, something that presented difficulty for her, since she was in unfamiliar surroundings. While flying she would sometimes become disoriented, as she would some afternoons in camp, believing she was back in her New York apartment. She would valiantly struggle with the bookkeeping chores, payroll, bills, etc., refusing to accept my quietly offered help and refusing to relinquish any of her pride and independence. After an hour of increasing frustration, she would get up from the table and say: "Livy, can you give me a hand?"

Allie would go out fishing in her canoe once or twice during these last three or four summers, if I would accompany her and her guide. She fished sitting down, still casting a nice line, but unable to see her fly, because of macular degeneration. Her last two summers, at age 94 and 95, she had a hard time staying warm, since she had become much more sensitive to even mildly cool weather and our only heat was from the fireplaces. Much of the time she spent wrapped in blankets on her favorite couch. It was getting difficult to mobilize her from couch or bed to get to meals. Those two

Katharine deB. Parsons, age 92, and Livy Parsons, age 64, at Boland Brook in 1989.

summers I slept in the room next to hers, so I could hear her when she needed help and so I could assist her in getting up at night. In 1937, I do not think either of us envisioned what the future would hold for the two of us.

In June of 1993, Joan and I left Albuquerque to go to New York City for our younger son, David's wedding. Of course, we spent as much time with Allie in her apartment as we could. At some time during this visit I knew a moment I had been dreading for several years had arrived, so gathering my courage I said, "Allie, there is something we need to talk about." I think she had been dreading this moment as I had, because, before I could say another word, she looked me in the eye and said, more as a statement than a question, "You are not going to take me to camp?" My response was, "I didn't say that, Allie, but it is getting harder to take care of you in Canada." Again, she interrupted me, "You are not going to take me to camp, are you?" "No," I said, "I am not." It was one of the saddest moments of my life.

During the next week she stopped eating, soon refusing to get out of bed, eventually refusing even liquids. In less than five days she peacefully passed away at the age of ninety-six. Her doctor could not point to anything physically wrong with her during these last days. She had lost her reason for living. There is a lot more I could say about this, but I think it would be superfluous. Our family lost an unusual, kind, generous and enterprising woman; she was loved.

Katharine deB. Parsons and Livy Parsons tackle the bookkeeping, 1989.

Conservation and Management

ince Allie's death I have undertaken the running of Boland Brook Camp and Wayne Borden of Upsalquitch has been Camp Manager and Head Guide.

Charlotte Borden, Wayne's sister-in-law, of Robinsonville has been our cook. Denis Arsenault of Point LaNim has been our second guide. Heather MacDougal, of Robinsonville, who has been with us for eighteen years is our girl Friday, and keeps the camp running smoothly. Everything else that needs to be done is done by Ernie Murray of Upsalquitch, who has grown from a boy to a man, while working at the camp. We have a happy, loyal, devoted and competent crew.

I retired from the practice of surgery in 1987 and Joan and I usually spend two months every summer at Boland Brook Camp, much to our satisfaction. Our two sons, Livy III and David, and often their wives, Mandy and Trish, have always spent a week with us at camp. Our daughter, Denise Parsons Rosson, and her husband Charlie Rosson, have always come from California for a week, but now with two small children, Charlie, as confirmed a salmon fisherman as the others, comes alone. It will not be long, however, before the fourth generation of Parsons' will be enjoying Boland Brook.

In the recent years, other camp owners have had more chances to meet, even though the camps are widely spread out along the river. We know many members of Camp Harmony at the mouth of the Upsalquitch, where it joins the Restigouche River, Rick and Beth Warren of Bangor, Maine, at Milbrook Farm, Tucker Cluett, now deceased, of Blue Hill, Maine, at MacClennan Lodge, and the Thompson family of Halifax, Nova Scotia, at Camp Watiqua. Boland Brook and Joe and Edgar Cullman's Two Brooks are the two up river camps. The Cullmans are from New York City and we see something, of each other every summer, but not as much as we would like.

I believe it was in the summer of 1985, when I was fishing in our Camp Pool with Wayne Borden, that a canoe, with a fisherman in a red-checked, wool jacket and a L.L. Bean hat, accompanied by his guide, Lee Marshall, stopped on their way up river and parked on the beach opposite us. After several minutes of scrutiny by our visitors, we became self-conscious and came ashore. That was the first time I met Joseph Cullman III, then President of the Atlantic Salmon Federation and one of the best friends ever of Atlantic salmon. From this meeting on the river, a firm friendship developed between Joe, myself and our two wives, both named Joan. Shortly thereafter Joe asked me if I would be interested in serving on the Board of the Atlantic Salmon Federation, an opportunity I declined, because I felt my busy surgical practice in Albuquerque would not allow me the time and effort I would want to devote to the ASF. I don't know how Joe knew the right time, but two weeks after I retired, he called to ask: "Are you ready?" My response was: "I am ready; put me to work."

One thing that has, unfortunately, changed for the worse over the years is the health of the spawning runs of Atlantic salmon in the Upsalquitch River. In the first half of the 20th century the size of the run was estimated at 10,000 fish. Historically, in the 19th century the estimated fish production for the Restigouche River system was 184,000 to 230,000 salmon, and it would be reasonable to expect that at least 10%, or 18,400 to 23,000, would have been Upsalquitch salmon and grilse. At this time salmon were believed to be unlimited in number and no one expected it to be otherwise at any time in the future. The Northwest branch of the Upsalquitch has a barrier holding pool ten miles up from where the river forks into Southeast and Northwest branches. Most of the spawning fish, 80%, turn right up the Northwest, so from fish counts in the barrier pool, where fish are trapped and held, and from radio tagging studies, the estimated run in the last ten years has been 2,000 to 2,200 fish, a five-fold decrease in my lifetime. During this time, commercial fishing on the high seas and offshore netting, with the exception of a subsistence fishery on the west coast of Greenland, have been eliminated by government regulation. Catch-and-Release has greatly reduced the number of fish removed from the river by recreational fishermen, and we know that under conditions of normal water temperature, 95% of released fish survive. So, what is going on? What is the problem?

Boland Brook Camp staff today: Denis Arsenault, Heather MacDougal, Ernie Murray, Charlotte Borden and Wayne Borden.

Something detrimental is going on in the North Atlantic, where salmon spend most of their life cycle, be it global warming, reduced forage fish lower in the food chain, an increase in the number of predators, increased mortality from spraying of nonyl-phenols into the rivers or a combination of all these factors. I am going to be outspoken, since, as you must know by now, I feel passionately about Atlantic salmon survival. I would have to put a large part of the blame for declining fish stocks on the provincial and federal governments; they have been reluctant to take needed preventative action and when they have acted to protect salmon stocks from depletion, it has been too little and too late. The common excuse is that there is not sufficient money available to do all that needs to be done. This is a strategy that results in decreasing income from the salmon resource to the province and a need for increased expenditure of funds in the future, when the situation has become critical and when more must be spent, with dollars that buy less, to support a resource that has further deteriorated.

The forest lands of the Northwest and Southeast Upsalquitch were opened to extensive timbering in the 1950s, '60s, '70s and '80s. On the Southeast branch, clear cutting was done, sometimes to the river edge and an extensive network of dirt roads and bridges was built, opening up inaccessible wilderness on both branches to poachers and others. When tree cutting was completed, the roads were never completely closed or removed, allowing easy access to the critical spawning areas, brooks and pools of the headwaters. Most of the poaching is done in the late summer and fall, when the water level is low and fish can be easily netted or scooped out. The Department of Natural Resources, which has management responsibility for hunting and fishing, could employ two or three extra wardens for the six weeks necessary to patrol these critical areas at the

Graph showing decline of salmon stocks in the North Atlantic. ICES stands for International Council for Exploration of the Seas. 2SW refers to adult salmon (not including grilse) that have spent two sea winters in the ocean.

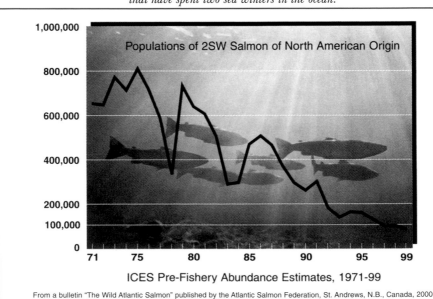

Populations of 2SW Salmon of North American Origin

ICES Pre-Fishery Abundance Estimates, 1971-99

From a bulletin "The Wild Atlantic Salmon" published by the Atlantic Salmon Federation, St. Andrews, N.B., Canada, 2000.

critical season. It has not. Furthermore, there has never been enough surveillance on the large stretches of public ("Crown") water to see that fishermen were properly licensed and were not removing more than their allowed limit of grilse. On the other hand, leased and owned stretches have always been well patrolled by the lessees and owners.

A flagrant example of poor management by Natural Resources occurred on the Boland Brook water in 1993. We caught two men illegally fishing in Josie's Pool. An untagged (tagging was required by law immediately after a catch) salmon was impaled on a stick by the shore and the men admitted to having hooked and lost another fish. They stated that they believed they were on their assigned stretch of Crown water, even though there was a large sign on a tree in full view of where they were fishing, which said in French and English: "Boland Brook, Private Property". Both men were from the local area, one knew the river well and both worked for the Department of Natural Resources. An immediate complaint was lodged with the regional Head Ranger in Campbellton and followed up with a letter to the Minister of Natural Resources in Fredericton, New Brunswick. The two men were not fired or even reprimanded; in fact,

PHOTO BY GENE SZERLIP

A salmon takes a dry fly in Josie's Pool in 1997.

the next day they were back fishing on the Crown water. If they had worked for you or me, what would have happened? Right! They would have been fired immediately. We have also found illegal nets and spinning tackle along the banks of Crown areas and everyone on the river has similar sad stories.

In the past, local Indian tribes have contributed to the problem of dwindling salmon stocks in the Upsalquitch. The Listiguj band of the Mi'kmaq First Nation has a reservation on the Quebec side of the Bay of Chaleur near the mouth of the Restigouche River. Using gillnets, that entangle and drown the big female spawners, as well as the smaller salmon and grilse, the Indians can effectively shut off the major portion of the fish about to ascend the Restigouche and its branches — the Upsalquitch, Matapedia,

Patapedia and Kedgwick rivers. No matter what limitations you impose on fishermen, even if all fish caught by fishermen were to be released, minimal spawning requirements cannot be met. if most of the spawners are netted out before they can enter the river. No one should deny the Indians a fair share of the salmon resource for subsistence and ceremonial purposes, but recently the Canadian government has reinforced the right of the Indians to sell wild salmon. Conservation groups have attempted to mitigate the effects of overzealous Indian netting by paying them not to fish on certain days or at certain times; effective, perhaps, on a short-term basis, but in the long run, bribery of this sort results in limited success, since the amount of a successful bribe always increases with time. This has happened. The Canadian government is going to have to gird up its loins and deal with these kinds of situations, before it is too late. Of all the players in the game of salmon conservation, the Indians have the most to lose, if the resource continues to be depleted.

The family today at Boland Brook, clockwise from top left: Livy Parsons, Livy Parsons III, Joan Parsons, David Parsons, Charlie Rosson and Denise Parsons Rosson. Photo taken in 1999.

It is encouraging that in recent years, the two local Indian bands are taking an increasingly responsible part, joining with other "user" groups to discuss and cooperate in salmon-conservation planning. The Atlantic Salmon Federation has played a major and ongoing role in getting the different groups to work together and to realize that they have a common goal. There is some hope for the future. Recent federal court decisions in Canada, the Sparrow Decision and the Marshall Decision, have reaffirmed Aboriginals' first right to use the salmon resource, providing the needs for conservation have been met. They also confirmed the right to use salmon, not just for subsistence and ceremonial purposes, but for commercial sale. I will say it once again; in enforcement of the conservation need, the Canadian government has not lived up to its responsibilities.

The Sparrow Decision granted Aboriginals rights to fish for salmon, essentially

Boland Brook today as it enters the Upsalquitch River at Boland Brook Camp. Photo taken in 2002.

without restriction, on private property or Crown water, without limitation as to time of year or the method of capture. Indians fish on Crown waters of the Upsalquitch, particularly in late summer and fall, often at times when non-Indians have reserved the water. Spinners, which are illegal for everyone else, are the usual method of fishing and it is estimated that in the last five years, 400 salmon and grilse were killed annually in this manner. Moreover, still another 200 to 250 fish are killed by non-Indian recreational anglers. If a maximum of 2,000 to 2,200 fish were entering the Upsalquitch to spawn, this would mean that almost 30% of the run was being killed annually, more, if you include poaching by non-Indians. These are rough estimates, but no river can maintain its health if this number of spawners are being taken. It is sad to see mismanagement of a healthy river. The Canadian government must develop some backbone if it is going to seriously combat depletion of a magnificent natural resource.

Boland Brook Camp will be starting its sixty-fourth year soon. Joan and I will be enjoying every minute that we spend there. So will our three children, Livy III, David and Denise, all of whom are excellent fishermen and conservationists. The summers spent at camp enable Joan and I to see not only our family, now spread from coast to coast, but also our hard-core fishing friends and our many New Brunswick friends, many of whom do or have worked for us. Boland Brook has been an important part of all our lives, supplying many wonderful experiences and memories. We hope many future generations will be enjoying the New Brunswick woods, our beautiful Upsalquitch River and the thrill of seeing the King of Game Fish, Atlantic salmon, jumping in our pools. The battle for salmon conservation and wise management must continue to be fought. It is a battle worth winning.

About the Author

Livingston Parsons Jr., age 77, is a retired general surgeon, living in Albuquerque, New Mexico, a graduate of Princeton University and Columbia University College of Physicians and Surgeons. He is a Clinical Professor of Surgery at The University of New Mexico School of Medicine and a Past President of the Southwestern Surgical Congress and of the Albuquerque and Bernalillo County Medical Association. He served in the Korean War in the Prisoner of War Command and as Chief of Surgery at the 48th MASH.

Dr. Parsons is a life-long trout and salmon fisherman. His wife, Joan, and their three children, Livy III, David and Denise P. Rosson, are also ardent fly-fishermen, particularly in so far as Atlantic salmon are concerned.

Dr. Parsons has long been a passionate advocate of salmon conservation, most notably in his activities with The Atlantic Salmon Federation as Chairman of its Research and Environment Committee since 1987. This has included directional input into the Federation's Salmon Genetic Research Program, creating a landmark study to document the effectiveness of catch-and-release angling and the promotion of Satellite Rearing, a method of raising young salmon out of harm's way near their native rivers. He has participated in three cooperative ventures with Moscow State University and The Wild Salmon Center of Seattle to study steelhead trout in Kamchatka, Russia.